Money Skills for Young Minds

An Essential and Fun Guide to Earning Money, Developing Budgeting Habits, and Spending Wisely

Catherine Louis

Contents

Introduction

Have you ever stared at your computer screen or the latest gadget and wished you had the money to buy it? You might be thinking to yourself, "Why didn't I save my allowance last week instead of blowing it all on candy?" Or, "What if I talk to my parents about doing more chores around the house to see if I can earn extra money?"

The purpose of this book is simple: to teach you the basics of financial literacy (the ability to understand and use various money skills) in a way that's fun and easy to understand. We'll break down big ideas into bite-sized pieces that you can chew on and enjoy. You'll learn how money works, how to earn it, how to budget, and how to save. We'll also talk about spending wisely and even how to invest money so it grows over time.

Why is financial literacy important for kids? Well, studies show that kids who learn about money early are more likely to make better financial decisions when they grow up. They're better at saving, budgeting, and even avoiding debt. Think of financial literacy like learning to ride a bike. The earlier you start, the better you get at it and the farther you can go.

Let's take a quick look at some of the cool topics we'll cover. First off, we'll learn about the basics of money—what it is and how it works. We'll talk about earning money, whether it's through chores, an allowance, or even starting a small business. You'll find out why saving is important and how to do it. We'll dive into budgeting so you know how to manage your money wisely. We'll also explore spending, investing, and even being generous with your money. Finally, we'll learn how to protect your money from being lost or stolen.

To make this journey even more exciting, we've included interactive elements like quizzes, activities, and practical exercises. These will help you practice what you've learned and make the process more fun. You'll find puzzles, games, and even some challenges that you can try with your family.

Speaking of family, this book isn't just for you. It's for your parents and grandparents, too. They can guide you through the lessons and share their own experiences with money. You can work on the activities together and discuss what you've learned. Trust me, it's a lot more fun when everyone gets involved.

Learning about money isn't just about numbers and math. It's about understanding how to make smart choices that will help you achieve your dreams. It's about feeling empowered and confident in your ability to manage your money. So, get ready to dive in and have some fun.

Please note: This book's information is general and designed for information only. While every effort has been made to ensure it is accurate, it is for general education purposes only and is not intended to be professional financial advice. The author and publisher are not responsible for any actions taken based on the information presented in this book.

Chapter 1

Understanding Money

When Charlie was around nine, he saved up all his birthday money because he had his eye on this awesome shiny bike at the store. Every time he walked by, he couldn't stop thinking about it. So, he saved every penny he could find. Finally, after weeks of saving, he marched into the store with his little wallet, ready to buy that bike! The clerk smiled at him and said, "Nice job saving up, kid!" His mom said that Charlie felt like a total rockstar that day. It wasn't just about the bike; it was about learning how to save and buy something by himself.

Money's a big deal in life, but it can also be pretty fun to learn about. The sooner you understand how it works, the better you'll be at saving and spending wisely. It's like learning to ride a bike—once you get the hang of it, you're good to go.

In this chapter, we'll chat about what money is and why it's important so you can get what you need (and want!) without worrying too much.

WHAT IS MONEY?

Money is anything we use to buy things like food, toys, or that cool bike you've been dreaming about. It comes in different forms—coins, bills, and even digital money you can use on your phone or computer.

Money is what you give to get things you need or want. It comes in different forms. We have coins that jingle in your pocket, paper bills that fold, and even digital money that you can't see but can use on your computer or phone.

Now, let's talk about what makes something "money."

1.   Money needs to be portable. That means it's easy to carry around.

Imagine trying to buy something with a cow. It wouldn't fit in your pocket, right? Coins and bills are small and light, making them easy to carry.

2.   Money needs to be durable. That means it has to last a long time.

Coins are made of metal, so they don't fall apart, and bills are made of special paper that doesn't tear easily. You wouldn't want your money to fall apart every time you take it out of your pocket.

3.   Money needs to be divisible. That means you can break it into smaller parts.

That means you can break it into smaller parts. For example, if you have a dollar, you can get four quarters, ten dimes, or twenty nickels. If you really wanted to, you could even get 100 pennies! This way, you can buy both big and small things.

4.   Money needs to be acceptable. That means everyone agrees to use it.

If you try to pay for something with a toy, the store clerk might look at you funny. But if you pay with coins or bills, everyone knows what it's worth.

Money's pretty cool because it has three main jobs.

·   It lets you buy stuff (medium of exchange)

· You can save it for later (store of value)

·   It helps you figure out how much things are worth (unit of account).

Without money, trading would be way harder—you'd have to swap things like sandwiches for apples all the time, which would be a mess!

THE HISTORY OF MONEY – FROM BARTER TO DIGITAL

Before there was money, people used something called bartering to trade goods and services. Imagine you had a cow and needed grain to feed your family. You'd find someone with grain who needed milk or beef, and you'd trade. Simple, right? But what if the grain owner didn't need a cow? You'd be out of luck. Bartering worked, but it wasn't always easy. People needed something everyone would accept, and that's where money came in.

Eventually, people came up with the idea of money—something everyone would accept in trade. First, there were coins made of precious metals like gold or silver.

Then, around the 7th century, people in China started using paper money because carrying around a ton of coins was annoying. Banks also popped up, helping people keep their money safe and introducing checks so people didn't have to carry all their cash around.

With the rise of technology, electronic banking emerged. Now, we can move money with just a few clicks on our computers or smartphones.

Nowadays, we've moved beyond coins and bills to digital money. You can buy stuff online with a click, use your phone to pay for snacks, and even get into cryptocurrencies like Bitcoin if you're feeling adventurous. It's like using virtual coins in a video game but for real stuff.

Different Forms of Money — Cash, Coins, and Digital

Cash is one of the most common forms of money you'll come across. Imagine folding a crisp dollar bill and tucking it into your wallet. That's cash. Paper bills, also known as notes, come in different denominations like $1, $5, $10, $20, $50, and $100. These bills are easy to carry and use for everyday purchases, like buying candy at the store or paying for a book at the school fair. You hand the cashier the right amount, and they will give you the change if needed. It's simple and straightforward.

Coins are another form of money that jingle in your pocket. They come in different denominations, too, like pennies, nickels, dimes, and quarters. Each coin is made of metal and has a unique design. For example, a penny is small and copper-colored, while a quarter is larger and silver. Coins are durable and last a long time. They're great for small purchases, like getting a gumball from a machine or paying for a bus ride. However, carrying a lot of coins can be heavy, and jingling all the time might get annoying.

Digital money is like the superhero of modern finance. You can't see or touch it, but it's there, making your life easier. Digital money includes debit and credit cards, mobile payments like Apple Pay and Google Wallet, and even cryptocurrencies like Bitcoin. With a debit card, you swipe or tap to pay, and the money comes straight out of your bank account. A credit card lets you borrow money to pay for things, and you pay it back later. Mobile payments let you use your phone to pay just by holding it near a payment terminal. Cryptocurrencies are digital coins you can use online. They're stored in digital wallets and can be used to buy things or trade.

Each type of money has its pros and cons. Cash is something you can touch and hold and is easy to understand. You can see it and feel it, making it great for learning about money. But it can be lost or stolen, and if you lose a bill, it's gone forever. Coins are durable and portable, perfect for small purchases. Yet, they can be heavy to carry in large amounts and might fall out of your pocket. Digital money is super convenient and secure. You can make payments quickly and keep track of your spending online. But it requires access to technology. If your phone dies or you lose your card, you might be stuck without money until you can get it sorted out.

Cash, coins, and digital money each play a role in our daily lives. They help us buy the things we need and want, from a candy bar at the store to a new game online. Understanding the different forms of money and how to use them can make managing your finances easier and more fun.

The Value of Money — Why It Matters

Understanding what gives money its value is like finding out why your favorite superhero is so powerful. Money gets its value from two main things: government backing and trust. Imagine if you tried to pay for a toy with a piece of paper you drew on. The store wouldn't accept it because it's not real money. Real money, like the dollar, is backed by the government. This means the government promises it's worth something. People trust this promise, so they accept dollars in exchange for goods and services.

Supply and demand also play a big role in the value of money. If there's too much money floating around, its value goes down. This is because everyone has money, so it's not as special. But if there's not enough money, its value goes up. Think of it like your favorite toy. If everyone has it, it's not as exciting. But if only a few people have it, it becomes more valuable. So, the government controls how much money is available to keep its value stable.

Now, let's talk about "purchasing power." This fancy term means how much you can buy with your money. If you have $1, you might be able to buy a candy bar today. But what if next year, that same candy bar costs $2? Your $1 won't stretch as far. This change happens because of inflation. Inflation is when prices go up, and your money buys less. On the flip side, deflation is when prices go down, and your money buys more. It's like a supersale where everything costs less.

Why is the value of money important for kids? Understanding this helps you make smarter choices, like saving now so you'll have more money for stuff in the future.

Money also helps in daily transactions. When you buy lunch at school or pay for a book at the store, you use money to get what you need. Knowing the value of money helps you make informed decisions. You'll understand why some things cost more and why it's important to save for bigger purchases. It's all about making the most of what you have and planning for what you want.

Money makes our lives easier. It helps us trade, buy, and save. Understanding its value is like having a superpower. You'll make better choices and feel more confident about your money. So next time you hold a dollar bill, remember it's not just a piece of paper. It's a tool that helps you get the things you need and want. Knowing how to use it wisely is one of the most important skills you can have.

NEEDS VS. WANTS – UNDERSTANDING PRIORITIES

When it comes to money, understanding the difference between needs and wants is super important. "Needs" are the things you can't live without, like food, clothes, or shelter. Without these, we can't survive. On the other hand, "wants" are things that are nice to have but not necessary. These include toys, games, and candy (the fun stuff).

For example, if you have $10 and need new shoes but want a toy, you should probably get the shoes first. The shoes are a need because your old ones have holes in them. The toy is a want. You have to choose. Needs should always come first because they are needed for living. Once your needs are taken care of, you can save up for the toy. It's all about making smart choices and learning to balance what's important.

Here's another example. Sam was at the store with his parents and saw a new video game he'd been dreaming about. But his mom reminded him that he needed a new jacket for winter. Sam has to choose. Making that choice wasn't easy. He had to choose between a warm jacket (a need) and a videogame (a want.) It might be tough, but choosing the jacket is the smart move. You need it to stay warm and healthy. The toy can wait. This is where the importance of saving comes in. If you save a part of your allowance, you can eventually buy the toy without affecting your needs. It's all about making smart choices and learning to balance what's important.

Budgeting is a great way to balance your needs and wants. Create a basic budget to divide your money wisely. Start by listing all your needs and their costs. This could include things like lunch money, school supplies, and clothing. Then, list your wants and their costs. Allocate, or set aside, money for your needs first. Once you've covered those, see how much you have left for your wants. Maybe you decide to save part of your allowance each week for a new game. This way, you're not spending all your money at once, and you're making sure your needs are met.

Let's break this down with an example. Imagine you get a $20 allowance each week. You need $10 for lunch money and school supplies. That leaves you with $10. You want a new toy that costs $30. Instead of spending all your leftover money on snacks or small treats, you decide to save $5 each week. In six weeks, you'll have enough to buy the toy. This way, you're prioritizing your needs and saving for your wants. It's a win-win!

Understanding the difference between needs and wants helps you make smarter choices with your money. It teaches you the value of saving and planning. It also helps you avoid spending all your money on things you don't really need, leaving you short on the important stuff. By learning to budget and prioritize, you'll be better prepared to manage your money now and in the future.

MONEY IN OUR DAILY LIVES – REAL-WORLD EXAMPLES

Money is something we use every day, even if we don't think about it much. Here's a simple example: buying lunch at school. When you pay with cash or a card, you're using money to get your food. Money keeps things running at school and at home, too. Your parents use it daily to pay for bills, groceries, and other things the family needs.

Some kids get a weekly allowance, and some don't. If you don't get an allowance, you can see if your parents will let you earn money by doing chores or small jobs, like mowing the lawn or washing the car. When you save that money in a piggy bank or account, you can watch it grow! Small amounts add up over time, and saving helps you buy things you want later on.

Try these activities to learn more about money:

- One fun way to understand needs and wants is to create a collage. Grab some old magazines, scissors, and glue. Cut out pictures of things you need and things you want. Make two sections on a piece of paper and glue the pictures in the right spots. This visual exercise helps you see the difference between the two and makes it easier to prioritize your spending.

- Another useful exercise is tracking your expenses for a week. Write down everything you spend money on, no matter how small. At the end of the week, review your list and see where your money went. This activity helps you understand your spending habits and see areas where you can save.

Money is a part of daily life for everyone. From buying lunch at school to parents paying bills and groceries, it's always in use. Earning money through chores or small jobs teaches you the value of hard work. Saving money in a piggy bank or savings account shows how small amounts can grow over time. Family finances might seem big and complicated, but they're just about making sure there's enough for everything the family needs. By budgeting and saving, families can meet their needs and still have money for fun and emergencies.

So, go ahead and try out these activities. Create your needs vs. wants collage and track your expenses for a week. These simple exercises will help you understand the value of money and how it fits into your daily life. Remember, money is more than just something adults deal with—it's a tool you can learn to use wisely now. And the more you practice, the better you'll get at making smart money choices!

Chapter 2

Earning Money

When I was a kid, I used to help my neighbor, Mrs. Verstegen, with her garden. She had the most beautiful flowers, and she needed someone to water them while she was away. She gave me a few dollars every week. I felt proud and excited because I earned that money myself. It made me realize the value of hard work and how I could make money by helping others.

What are some ways you can start earning money at home? One of the easiest ways to get started is by doing chores. Chores are simple tasks around the house that help keep everything running smoothly. Think about washing dishes, taking out the trash, or even making your bed. These tasks might seem small, but they make a big difference. Kids of all ages can do chores. Younger kids might put their toys away or help feed the family pet. Older kids might take on bigger tasks like vacuuming or helping cook dinner.

Consistency is key when it comes to chores. Make sure chores are done regularly, whether they're daily or weekly tasks. Daily chores could include making the bed or feeding the pet. Weekly chores might be vacuuming or mowing the lawn. Creating a chore chart can help keep track of everything. List the chores, who's responsible, and when they need to be done. This way, everyone knows what's expected, and, as I remember, with my own kids, it saves a lot of arguing!

Creating a chore chart is a great way to stay organized. Here's a simple format you can use:

Task	Who	When
Make your bed	Jamie, Alex	Daily
Wash the dishes	Jamie	Daily
Sweep the floor	Alex	Daily
Take out the trash	Alex	Wednesday
Vacuum the living room	Jamie	Saturday

This chart helps everyone stay on track and makes it clear who's responsible for what.

Talk to your parents. Maybe they can set up an allowance system to reward you for doing your chores. An allowance is money that kids get for completing their tasks. It teaches you that hard work pays off. To start, decide on a fair amount for each chore. For example, you might get $1 for taking out the trash or $2 for washing the dishes. Keep track of completed chores using a chore chart. Write down each task and mark it off when it's done. This helps everyone see what's been accomplished and what still needs to be done.

You may not do the task perfectly at first. Make sure you understand the job and do your best. The goal is to teach responsibility, not to have everything done perfectly. Over time, with practice, kids get better at their tasks.

Earning money through chores is a great way for kids like you to learn about the value of work and responsibility. It helps you understand that money doesn't just appear out of nowhere; it takes effort and dedication to earn it.

When you complete your chores, you realize that you have an important role in the family. If chores aren't done, there should be consequences. Maybe you lose some allowance or have to do an extra task. On the flip side, consistent performance should be rewarded. Maybe you could be a little extra allowance or a special treat. So, grab a chore chart, talk to your parents, and start deciding on those tasks!

STARTING A LEMONADE STAND – BASICS OF A SMALL BUSINESS

Starting a lemonade stand is a fun way to learn about money and business. Here are some steps to get you started,

First, plan where to set up. A busy street corner or park is a good choice—make sure to get permission if needed. Choose a date and time, like a sunny afternoon on the weekend, when people are out and might want a cold drink.

Make a plan to get your supplies. You'll need lemons, sugar, water, and ice to keep your lemonade cold. Write down the cost of each item so you know how much money you need to start and how much you need to earn back. You'll also need a pitcher, cups, and a table to put your things on.

Once you have your supplies, you can set up your stand. Adding colorful signs and a tablecloth can make your stand look more inviting.

Setting a fair price is important. Try starting at 50 cents or a dollar per cup. You could also offer deals, like buy one, get one free, to get more people to buy.

When customers come by, greet them with a smile. Being polite and friendly makes people want to buy from you again.

Running a lemonade stand teaches you about profit (money you make after covering costs) and loss (when you spend more than you earn). Keep track of what you earn and spend to see how well you're doing. Good customer service—like saying "thank you" or asking how someone's day is going—makes people happy and more likely to return.

Managing the money you make is also part of the experience. Keep your earnings in a safe place, like a cash box, and track how much you make. You can save some money for your next stand or for something you really want.

A lemonade stand isn't just about making money; it's about learning skills like planning, budgeting, and running a small business. Plus, you get to spend time outside and meet new people. So, grab some lemons, set up your stand, and start your business adventure. You'll have fun, learn a lot, and might even make some cash!

Pet Sitting and Dog Walking – Fun Jobs for Kids

Pet sitting and dog walking can be a fun way to earn money. Start by letting your neighbors, family, and friends know you're offering pet care services. You can tell them in person or make simple flyers listing what you do, like feeding pets, walking dogs, or cleaning litter boxes. Make sure to include your contact info so they can reach you. You can also ask your parents to help share your services on community boards or social media so more people find out.

Taking care of pets is a big responsibility. Each pet needs different things to stay happy and healthy. For example, dogs need walks, food, and playtime. Cats might need their litter box cleaned and fresh water every day. Always ask the pet owner for any special instructions or about any health issues their pet has. This helps you know exactly what to do and how to keep each pet safe. When walking dogs, use a leash and avoid strange animals. If a dog seems scared or aggressive, steer clear to stay safe.

Setting a schedule and rates is important. Decide on a routine for each pet, like walking dogs once a day or a few times a week. Pick a fair price for each visit or walk, like $5 for a walk or $10 per hour. Keep a calendar to track appointments so you don't forget any.

Being on time and dependable is key to earning trust. If you promise to arrive at 3 PM, be there at 3 PM. Pet owners appreciate reliability and are more likely to hire you again. Send updates to pet owners, like a quick message or photo of their pet on a walk, to show you're taking good care of them. Don't be afraid to ask for feedback or referrals. Happy clients might tell friends about you, helping you get more business.

Pet sitting and dog walking teach important skills like responsibility, time management, and money handling. You learn how to keep a schedule, organize your work, and make some money. Plus, you get to spend time with animals, whether it's playing with dogs, cuddling cats, or even caring for rabbits or birds. It's a fun way to earn money while doing something you enjoy.

So, if you like animals and want to earn some cash, consider starting a pet-sitting and dog-walking business. It's a great way to build skills and have fun with furry friends. Just remember to be safe, responsible, and reliable—your neighbors and their pets will thank you!

CRAFT SALES – TURNING HOBBIES INTO EARNINGS

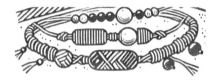

Craft sales are a great way to make money from hobbies you enjoy. Think about crafts you like making, like friendship bracelets, painted rocks, or handmade cards. Friendship bracelets are popular and easy to make, painted rocks can be used as decorations, and unique cards are perfect for birthdays or holidays. Pick crafts you're good at and enjoy making so people will be excited to buy them.

Setting up a spot to sell your crafts is important. You could start by selling at community fairs or markets, where lots of people come to check things out. Ask your parents if there are any local events you can join. Another option is to set up an online store. With your parents' help, you can use sites like Etsy to show off your crafts. Take good photos, write clear descriptions, and include prices so people know what they're buying.

To price your crafts, think about the cost of materials. Add up how much you spent on supplies, like beads for bracelets or paint for rocks. Then, add a bit more to make a profit. For example, if a bracelet costs $1 to make, you might sell it for $3 to cover costs and earn some money. Keep prices fair; if they're too high, people might not buy, and if they're too low, you might not make enough.

Marketing your crafts helps you sell more. With your parents' supervision, you can post photos of your crafts on social media and let people know where they can buy them. Telling friends, family, and neighbors also helps spread the word. Make sure your display looks good, too. Arrange your crafts nicely, use signs to show prices, and maybe even add some special offers. The better your setup looks, the more likely people are to stop by.

Selling crafts teaches useful skills like planning, budgeting, and marketing. You also get better at talking to customers and handling money. Each sale builds your confidence and shows that people like what you make. Plus, making crafts is fun and lets you be creative.

If you love making crafts, give it a shot! Pick your favorite craft, set up your shop, and start selling. You'll learn a lot, have fun, and might even make some extra money. Plus, you'll get to share your creations with others. So gather your supplies, start crafting, and show the world what you can make!

YARD WORK – HELPING NEIGHBORS AND EARNING CASH

Yard work is a good way to earn money while helping your neighbors. There are a few types of yard work you can offer. Mowing lawns means using a lawnmower to cut grass evenly, which takes effort to do well. Raking leaves is another job. In fall, leaves pile up and need to be gathered and bagged. Watering plants with a hose or watering can also keep them healthy. These tasks keep yards looking nice.

To get started, ask your parents if it's okay to offer your services to neighbors. Then, politely let neighbors know what you can do. Try saying, "Hi, I'm Jamie from down the street. I can help with mowing, raking, and watering. Would you be interested?" Give them your contact info, maybe on a flyer, along with your name, number, and services. Being polite and clear builds trust.

Setting prices and a schedule is important to stay organized. You could charge per task or by the hour, like $10 to mow a lawn or per hour for raking leaves. Keep a schedule so you don't overcommit. Write down when you're free to work so you and your neighbors can plan ahead. Doing a few jobs well is better than rushing through too many.

Safety is key in yard work. Use tools that are right for your age. Younger kids can start with simple tasks like watering and raking, while older kids may use lawnmowers. Wear safety gear like gloves to protect your hands and goggles to protect your eyes from sticks or stones. Don't work in extreme heat—take breaks and drink water. Staying safe keeps yard work fun.

It's important to know how to use tools. Ask an adult to show you how to use a lawnmower safely or how to handle rakes and hoses. Using tools correctly prevents accidents and helps you do a good job. If you're unsure about a tool, always ask for help.

Yard work teaches responsibility and pride in doing a good job. When you finish mowing or cleaning a yard, you see the results of your work. Happy neighbors might even tell others about your services, helping you grow your business. It's a win-win—you make money, learn skills, and make your neighborhood look nice.

So put on your gloves, grab a rake, and start offering your yard work services. Each task, whether it's mowing, raking, or watering, helps you grow and learn. Plus, you get to earn some money along the way!

The Importance of Earning — Learning Responsibility

Earning money through work is important because it helps you understand the value of hard work. Imagine saving up for a new game or toy. When you finally have enough to buy it, you appreciate it more because you know the effort it took to earn that money. This feeling of accomplishment comes from knowing that money isn't just given to you; you have to work for it. When you earn money yourself, you learn to take better care of the things you buy.

Setting personal goals is also important when earning money. Goals give you something to work toward and keep you motivated. For example, if you want to save for a new bike, start by setting a specific goal. Write down how much you need, then plan how to earn it. You could do extra chores, start a small business, or find weekend jobs. Having a clear goal makes it easier to stay focused and teaches you how to manage your money to reach it.

Earning money also helps you learn money management skills. When you have your own money, you have to decide how to use it. Try making a simple budget by dividing your money into different categories. You might save some, spend some, and share or donate some. For example, if you earn $20, you could save $10, spend $5, and donate $5. This helps you learn how to balance spending, saving, and planning for the future.

One of the best parts of earning money is how it makes you feel more confident and independent. When you work and earn, you feel proud of your accomplishments. This confidence grows as you learn to manage your money and make choices about spending and saving. Being able to say, "I earned this money and decided how to use it," shows that you are responsible and capable.

Earning money also helps you build a strong work ethic. You learn that putting in effort leads to rewards. Whether you're doing chores, running a small business, or taking on jobs, the work you put in reflects the results you get. This lesson is helpful not only for earning money but also for school, sports, and other areas of life. A strong work ethic teaches you the value of persistence.

For example, imagine you set a goal to save $50 for a new video game. You decide to earn this by doing extra chores at home and offering yard work to neighbors. Each week, you earn a few dollars and save it. After a few months, you reach your goal and buy the game. The satisfaction isn't just about having the game; it's about knowing you worked hard to reach your goal. This shows that with effort and determination, you can achieve what you want.

Earning money isn't just about getting cash. It's about learning responsibility, setting goals, managing money, and building confidence. As you keep earning and learning, you'll become more independent and able to make smart financial decisions. Next, we'll explore the world of saving money and how it can help you reach even bigger goals.

Chapter 3

Saving Money

Do you have a piggy bank? Or, maybe it's more of a small locked box. Where do you keep the coins and dollars that you save? Your parents are probably the ones who encourage you to save your money, But do you know why?

THE CONCEPT OF SAVING – WHY SAVE MONEY?

Saving money means putting aside some of what you earn to use in the future. It's like keeping a little stash for your future self. Instead of spending all your money right away, you keep some in a safe place.

This way, when you need or want something special, you already have money saved up. Think of it as a backup fund for when something unexpected happens.

Saving money is helpful for a few reasons. First, it helps you be ready for surprise costs. Imagine you're saving up for a new scooter, but your favorite toy breaks and needs to be replaced. With savings, you can fix the toy without giving up on your scooter goal. Saving also helps you reach bigger goals, like buying a game console or helping with a family trip. By saving regularly, you can make those bigger goals happen.

Here are some examples of saving.

Let's say there's a scooter at the store you really want, and it costs $100. Instead of spending all your allowance on snacks or small toys, you decide to save $10 each week. In 10 weeks, you'll have enough for the scooter.

Or maybe your family is planning a beach vacation. You could save part of your allowance each week to have spending money for the trip. When the time comes, you'll have cash ready for fun activities or souvenirs.

Saving money has a lot of benefits. One big benefit is feeling secure because you know you have money for emergencies or unexpected costs. It's like having a safety net. Another benefit is that you can reach personal goals, like getting that new scooter or enjoying a special trip. When you finally reach your goal, you feel proud because you know it's thanks to your hard work and patience.

Saving also teaches you useful life skills. You learn how to set goals, manage money, and make smart choices. These skills are important and will help you in the future. Plus, watching your savings grow over time is pretty cool and can even be fun. It's like watching a plant grow from a small seed into a big tree.

To make saving more fun, try a savings challenge. Make a chart to track your progress and color in a section each week as you save more. This helps you see how close you are to your goal and keeps you motivated. You can also share your goals with your family, who might even join you with their own savings goals. It can become a fun family activity.

Saving money is a powerful habit that helps you reach your goals and gives you a sense of accomplishment. Start setting aside some of your money today and watch your savings grow. Every little bit counts, and before you know it, you'll reach your goals and feel the rewards of your hard work and smart saving.

Piggy Banks and Saving Jars – Fun Ways to Save

When my younger daughter was a kid, her favorite way to save money was with a piggy bank. A piggy bank is a small container, often shaped like a pig, where you can put coins and small bills. It's a fun and visual way to watch your savings grow. Every time you drop a coin into the piggy bank, you hear a satisfying clink. It's like adding a piece to a puzzle, knowing that over time, those small pieces will turn into something big.

Another great way to save money is to use different types of saving jars. You can have separate jars for different purposes. One jar can be for spending, another for saving, and a third for sharing.

·   The spending jar holds money you plan to use soon, such as to buy a small toy or a treat.

·   The savings jar holds money you want to set aside for bigger purchases, like a new bike or game console.

·   The sharing jar is for money you want to give to others, such as by donating to a charity or buying a gift for someone special.

Having different jars helps you see where your money is going and makes saving more organized and fun.

Decorating your piggy banks and jars can make saving even more enjoyable. Grab some paint, stickers, and markers, and let your creativity flow. You can paint your piggy bank in your favorite colors or decorate it with fun designs. Label your jars with their purposes using colorful markers. Write "Spending," "Saving," and "Sharing" on each jar so you know what each one is for. Personalizing your savings tools makes them special and motivates you to use them more.

Tracking your savings progress is important to see how close you are to reaching your goals. One way to do this is by using a savings chart. Draw a chart with sections that represent different amounts of money. Every time you add money to your piggy bank or jars, color in a section of the chart. This chart helps you see your progress and keeps you motivated. Another way to track your savings is by counting your money regularly. Set a time each week to count the money in your piggy bank and jars. Write down the amounts and see how much you've saved. This practice helps you stay on top of your savings and shows you how quickly small amounts can add up.

SAVINGS CHART EXAMPLE

Creating a savings chart can be a fun and motivating way to track your progress. Here's a simple example:

My Savings Chart

Date	$ Saved	Total Savings
Jan. 1	$5	$5
Jan. 8	$3	$8
Jan. 15	$7	$15
Jan. 22	$4	$19

Every week, add the amount you've saved and update your total savings. Seeing the numbers grow will encourage you to keep saving.

Saving money doesn't have to be boring. With piggy banks and saving jars, you can make it a fun and creative activity. Watching your money grow over time gives you a sense of achievement and teaches you the value of saving. So, grab a piggy bank or some jars, start decorating, and begin your savings adventure. You'll be surprised at how quickly your small efforts can lead to big rewards.

SETTING SAVINGS GOALS – PLANNING FOR THE FUTURE

Setting a savings goal is like creating a plan. It shows you the steps to take and helps you know where you're going. A savings goal is a clear target you want to reach, like saving $50 for a new game or $100 for a bike. Goals are important because they give you something to work toward. Without a goal, saving can feel like going in circles with no end. But when you know exactly what you're saving for, it's easier to stay motivated and keep adding to your savings.

There are two main types of savings goals: **short-term** and **long-term**.

- Short-term goals are things you can achieve in a few weeks or months.

For example, saving for a toy or game is a short-term goal. You might save a bit of your allowance each week and reach your goal in a couple of months.

- Long-term goals take more time and planning.

Saving for college or a car falls into this category. These goals might take years to achieve, but they are worth it in the end. Understanding the difference between short-term and long-term goals helps you plan better and stay focused.

Setting a savings goal starts with deciding what you want to save for. It could be a new skateboard, a trip to an amusement park, or even a car when you turn sixteen. Once you know what you want, figure out how much money you'll need. If the skateboard costs $50, that's your target. Next, set a timeline for reaching your goal. Decide how long you'll take to save the money. If you want the skateboard in five months, plan how much you need to save each week. Breaking it down like this makes it easier. Saving $10 each month sounds more doable than thinking about the full $50 at once.

As you work toward your goal, reward yourself when you hit milestones. Small rewards keep you motivated and make saving fun. For example, if you're saving $100 in six months, celebrate when you reach $25, $50, and$75. These rewards could be a favorite snack or a fun activity with family or friends. Getting your family involved in your goals can make saving even better. Talk to your parents or grandparents about what you're saving for. They might have helpful ideas or ways to help you earn extra money, like extra chores or small neighborhood jobs. Having their support and advice makes reaching your goals easier and more fun.

A great way to track your savings is to use a visual tracker. Create a chart with sections for different amounts and color in a section each time you save. It's like watching your progress come to life. You can also use apps or online tools to track your savings, which let you set goals, track progress, and even earn virtual rewards. Seeing your progress helps you stay on track and makes saving more exciting. **See Appendix A at the end of the book for a sample of a visual savings tracker.**

Reaching your savings goals teaches you important lessons about planning, patience, and sticking with it. It shows that with a clear plan and steady effort, you can reach your dreams. Start setting your savings goals today. Decide what you want, figure out how much you need, and set a timeline. Track your progress, celebrate your achievements, and keep at it. With determination and planning, you'll reach your goals and enjoy the rewards of your hard work.

This link can open up other savings charts for you. https://www.101plan ners.comBe sure to check with your parents before downloading anything.

DELAYED GRATIFICATION – THE POWER OF PATIENCE

Delayed gratification means "wait now, enjoy later." It's about holding off on something you want now so you can have something better in the future. For example, if you have money, you might be tempted to spend it all on candy. But if you save it, you could buy something bigger, like a new skateboard or a special outing with your family. It's about being patient and knowing that waiting can lead to better rewards.

There are a lot of benefits to waiting before spending. One big benefit is that you can make better purchases. Instead of buying small things right away, you can save and buy something that will last longer and make you happier. Another benefit is the feeling of satisfaction. When you finally get what you've been saving for, it feels even better because you waited for it.

Here are some examples. Let's say you see a cheap toy at the store, and you want to buy it right away. But then you remember there's a better version of that toy that costs a bit more. If you wait and save your money, you can buy the better version that will last longer and give you more fun.

Another example is saving for a special outing. Maybe you want to go to an amusement park with your friends. Instead of spending money on small treats and toys, you save up to buy tickets for the park and enjoy a day of rides and fun with your friends. Practicing patience can be challenging, but there are activities that can help.

- Wait a week before spending your saved money. When you get your allowance or earn some money from chores, set it aside and wait a week before deciding what to do with it. This helps you think carefully about your purchases and avoid impulse buys.

- Set up a reward system for waiting. Create a chart with different milestones and rewards. For example, if you wait a week before spending, you get a small reward like a favorite treat. If you wait a month, you get a bigger reward, like a fun outing or a special activity with your family. Ask your parents to help you with this.

So, the next time you feel the urge to spend right away, take a deep breath, think about what you really want, and remember that good things come to those who wait.

Saving vs. Spending — Making Smart Choices

Saving and spending are two sides of the same coin. Saving means putting money aside for future use—like planting seeds that will grow into a big tree. Spending, on the other hand, is using money to buy goods or services now. Think of it as picking fruit from a tree to enjoy right away. Understanding the difference helps you make smart choices about your money.

Thinking before you spend is important. Remember our discussion of **Needs and Wants** from the first chapter? Before you buy something, ask yourself if it's a need or a want. Needs are things you must have, like food and clothes. Wants are things that are nice to have, like toys and games. Consider if you can afford it without affecting your savings goal. If buying that new toy means you won't have enough money for a school trip, waiting might be better. Think about what matters more to you in the long run.

Creating a spending plan helps you balance saving and spending. You can start by dividing your allowance into different parts, as we mentioned before – one part for saving, one for spending, and one for sharing. This way, you can enjoy some of your money now while still putting some aside for the future. And remember to track your expenses. When you write down what you spend each week, you can see where your money goes and avoid overspending. It's like having a map that guides you on your money journey.

Smart spending tips help you get more for your money. Look for sales and discounts—buying things on sale means you spend less and save more. Compare prices before buying; the same item might cost less at a different store. Avoid impulse buys, which are things you buy without thinking. Take a moment to ask if you really need it or if you can wait. This helps you make thoughtful choices and avoid wasting money.

Imagine you have $20 at the toy store and see an action figure for $15. Before you buy, think about your savings goal. You're saving for a bike that costs $100. If you spend $15 now, you'll have less for your bike. Is the action figure a need or a want? Can you wait and save the $ 15 instead? These questions help you decide if it's worth it. Maybe you decide to wait for the bike or find the same figure on sale for $10 somewhere else. Smart choices help you make the most of your money.

Parents and grandparents can help teach these tips. Talk with them about saving versus spending and ask them to share their experiences. They can help you make a spending plan and track your expenses. Learning to look for deals and think before buying will help you build smart money skills.

Smart spending is a skill that takes practice. Start by understanding the difference between saving and spending. Think about your purchases, make a spending plan, and use smart tips to get the best value. With these tools, you'll enjoy your money now and in the future.

OPENING A SAVINGS ACCOUNT – FIRST STEPS TO BANKING

Opening a savings account is a cool way to start learning about money. A savings account is a safe place to keep your money. Instead of putting it in a piggy bank, you put it in a bank where it's protected. The best part? Your money can earn interest, which is like a bonus the bank gives you for keeping your money with them. Over time, your savings can grow without adding more money—just like watching a plant grow.

Ask your parents to help you choose the right bank for your savings account. Look for kid-friendly banks. Some offer accounts for kids with no fees, so there's no cost to keep money there. You could also check out local credit unions or online banking options, where you can easily check balances and track savings on a computer or smartphone.

Opening a savings account is simple. Your parent will need to help you fill out some forms. When you get to the bank, tell the bank worker you want to open a savings account. They'll help you through the steps. Then, make your first deposit—it could be just $5 or $10. Now, congratulations! You have a savings account.

Managing your account is important. Start by regularly checking your balance to see how your money is growing. Most banks send monthly statements, which show you how much money you have. Ask a parent to help you read these statements to understand how your savings add up.

Having a savings account teaches you responsibility. You'll learn to keep track of your money and make smart choices about when to save and when to spend. Watching your savings grow over time can be exciting and shows you that saving is worth it. You'll feel proud knowing you're building good money habits for the future.

Opening a savings account is a big step toward being financially independent. It gives you a safe place for your money and helps it grow with interest. Choosing the right bank, learning to manage the account, and keeping track of your money are all part of the experience. These are skills you'll use for life, so take that first step, open a savings account, and start watching your money grow.

Chapter 4

Budgeting Basics

R emember in the last chapter I told you that I got a small weekly allowance when I was growing up? Well, instead of spending it all on candy and toys, I had a little notebook where I wrote down what I earned and what I spent. I didn't know it at the time, but I was learning how to budget. It was like a secret power that helped me save for things I really wanted. Today, I want to share that secret with you.

WHAT IS A BUDGET? — UNDERSTANDING THE BASICS

A budget is like a plan for your money. It tells you how much money you have coming in and how much you can spend or save. Think of it as a map that guides you on how to use your money wisely. A budget helps you avoid overspending and ensures you have enough money for the things you need.

Let's break down the main parts of a budget.

· The first part is **income**. Income is the money you earn or receive. It could come from an allowance, doing chores, or even running a lemonade stand. Income is the starting point of your budget because it shows how much money you have to work with.

· Next, we have **expenses**. These are the things you spend your money on. Expenses can be anything from buying snacks at school to saving for a new toy. It's important to list all your expenses so you can see where your money is going. This list helps you make better decisions about what to buy and what to save for later.

· The last part is **savings**. This is the money you set aside for future use. Savings are very important because they help you meet bigger goals and prepare for unexpected expenses. Imagine you're saving for a new bike. By setting aside a little bit of money each week, you'll eventually have enough to buy that bike. Savings also give you a safety net for emergencies, like when your favorite toy breaks and needs to be replaced.

Now, why is budgeting important?

Budgeting helps you avoid overspending. When you have a budget, you know exactly how much money you can spend. Budgeting prevents you from buying things you don't need and running out of money for the things you do need.

Budgeting makes sure you have money available for important needs. Whether you're saving for a big purchase or setting aside money for school supplies, a budget helps you plan ahead and stay prepared.

Let's look at some real-life examples of budgeting in everyday life. Imagine you get a weekly allowance of $10. You decide to budget your money by setting aside $5 for savings, $3 for spending, and $2 for sharing or donating. This way, you can save for something big, enjoy some small treats, and still help others. Another example is planning a budget for a school project. Let's say you need to buy materials for a science fair project. You make a list of everything you need, like poster boards, markers, and glue. Then, you check the prices and figure out how much money you need. This helps you make sure you have enough money and don't overspend.

Budgeting is a powerful tool that helps you manage your money wisely. It gives you control over your finances and helps you make smart choices. By understanding the basics of budgeting, you can start planning your money and reach your financial goals. So grab a notebook, start writing down your income and expenses, and watch how budgeting can make a big difference in your life.

CREATING A SIMPLE BUDGET – STEP-BY-STEP GUIDE

Setting up a budget might sound tricky, but it's easier than you think. Here are the steps-

1.   Write down your income. What is your income?

Income is the money you earn or receive. Think about all the ways you can make money. You might get an allowance for doing chores around the house. Maybe you earn a few dollars mowing the lawn or washing the car. Maybe you set up a lemonade stand on a sunny day and have a good turnout. Each of these is a source of income. Write down all the ways you earn money and how much you get from each one. Writing how you earn money helps you see how much you have to work with.

2.   Write down your expenses. What are your expenses?

These are all the things you spend money on. Start with your daily expenses like lunch money or snacks. Next, think about your weekly expenses. Maybe you spend money on hobbies or activities like buying art supplies or paying for a sports club. Don't forget about monthly expenses. Are you saving up for a big purchase, like a new toy or game? Write that down, too. Listing all your expenses helps you see where your money goes. It also helps you find areas where you might be able to save a little more.

 Once you have your income and expenses listed, it's time to think about savings.

3.   What do you want to save for?

Saving money is important because it helps you reach bigger goals and prepares you for unexpected expenses. Decide how much of your income you want to save each week. Maybe you set aside $2 from your allowance or earnings. You can use a savings jar or open a savings account at a bank. Putting money into savings regularly helps it grow over time. It's like planting seeds that will grow into a big tree.

4.   Balance your budget.

Your total income should equal your total expenses plus your savings. This means you're using all your money wisely without spending more than you make. If your expenses are higher than your income, you'll need to make some changes. Check your list of expenses and see where you can spend less. Maybe buy fewer snacks or find a cheaper hobby. Adjusting your budget helps you stay on track and make sure you have enough money for what you need.

Budget Worksheet

Creating a budget worksheet can help you organize your income, expenses, and savings. Here's a simple example:

My Budget Worksheet

Category	Income	Notes	Expenses	Notes	Savings	Notes
Weekly allowance from chores	$10					
lemonade-stand earnings	$5					
Lunch money			$5	School lunch		
Art Supplies			$3	Hobby expense		
Entertainment					$7	New toy
Total	$15	Equals	$8	Plus	$7	

In this example, you can see that we have a balanced budget—this means you're using all your money wisely without spending more than you make. Using a worksheet like this helps you see everything in one place. It makes budgeting simpler and more organized. You can update it each week to track your progress and make adjustments as needed.

Balancing your budget might take some practice, but it's worth it. It helps you make the most of your money and reach your goals. Plus, it's a great skill that will help you throughout your life. So grab a notebook, write down your income and expenses, and start creating your budget today. You'll be amazed at how much control you have over your money and how quickly you can reach your financial goals.

Track Your Spending – Keeping an Eye on Money

Tracking your spending is like being a detective with your money. It helps you see where all your money is going and makes sure you're not spending too much. Imagine you get some allowance, and by the end of the week, you don't know where it went. That's why tracking is important. It shows you exactly what you spent on snacks, toys, or games. This way, you can make better choices and avoid running out of money when you really need it. There are different ways to track your spending, and you can choose the best option.

- **A notebook**- Write down everything you buy each day. It could be as small as a candy bar or as big as a new game. By the end of the week, you'll have a clear picture of where your money went.

- If you like drawing and coloring, creating a **spending tracker chart** can be fun. Make a chart with sections for each type of expense, like snacks, toys, and some time savings. Color in each section as you spend money. It's a fun and visual way to keep track.

- **A budgeting app**. Some apps are made just for kids and can help you keep track of your spending with your parent's help. These apps can even show you cool graphs and charts to visualize your spending.

Here are some **budgeting apps for kids:**

- **goHenry**

  ○ This is a debit card financial app for kids ages 6 to 18. GoHenry is an allowance management app for kids and teens. Each kid in your family gets an individual bank account with a debit card. Parents control how and when kids can use the debit card and can see their running bank balance. Parents create the chores and allowance amounts, set spending limits, and get push alerts when children use debit cards.

- **FamZoo**

  ○ This app allows kids to manage money in savings, spending, and giving accounts. Famzoo is a prepaid **debit card for kids** and an allowance app that handles the family's finances. In addition, parents have a 'Parent Funding Card' that they can use to transfer funds to kids' prepaid cards instantly. You can send money for chores, compound interest, rewards, or money requests made in the app.   Kids can also send parents money for missed chores, family bill sharing, or loan interest.

- **Rooster Money (https://roostermoney.com)**

  ○ This is a prepaid debit card for kids, with a pocket money app and chore manager for ages 6-17.

- **Greenlight-**

  ○ Both you and your kids download the Greenlight app, which offers tailored experiences. Your kids check off chores, and you automate the allowance. You spend wisely, and you set flexible controls. Your kids build healthy financial habits, and you cheer them on.

- **Current**

  ○ This is an excellent debit card option for teens. It can be used anywhere Visa is accepted, but parents can control where teens spend their money and how much they spend. Parental controls help teens learn to save, spend, and give money; parents can help kids learn by managing where they spend.

- **Homey**

  ○ The Homey allowance app helps kids learn how to work for their earnings. With Homey, kids learn how to work toward what they want by setting goals and working toward them. You can transfer the funds earned directly to their checking or savings account, helping them learn how to manage their funds. The   Homey app alerts family members when chores are due or when someone completes their chores. It keeps everyone on the same page and helps the family work toward their financial goals.

- **iAllowance**

  - iAllowance is a simple app to track and pay for your child's chores. It's only available on iOS, and you can set the chore frequency and automatic transfers. For example, link your **child's bank account** and set up times for automatic withdrawals, or you can handle them manually. The app keeps track of all chores completed and money earned and spent, and you always know your child's financial situation with a quick look at the dashboard.

- **BusyKid**

  - This is an app and a VISA® prepaid card that helps kids learn how to earn, save, donate, and invest their allowance. Parents can set chores, monitor transactions, and transfer funds anytime and anywhere.

Checking your spending each week is a good habit. Take a few minutes to look at what you spent money on. This helps you see where your money is going. Maybe you realize you're buying too many snacks and not saving enough. Noticing these things helps you change how you spend. For example, if you spend $5 on snacks each week, try cutting it to $3 and saving the extra $2.

Spending Tracker Exercise

To help you get started with tracking, try this simple exercise. Create a spending tracker chart with columns for the date, item bought, and amount spent. Here's a basic example:

EXPENSE TRACKER

DATE	AMOUNT	CATEGORY	WANT OR NEED
May 3	$ 2.50	candy	want
May 4	$ 3.00	notebook	need
May 7	$ 2.00	pack of gum	want
May 11	$15.00	Mom b-day gift	need
Total wants-	$4.50		
Total needs-	$ 18.00		

At the end of the week, add up all the amounts to see your total spending. This exercise helps you see where your money goes and makes it easier to adjust your spending habits.

Tracking your spending is a powerful tool that helps you manage your money better. It shows you where your money is going and helps you avoid overspending. By using methods like a notebook, budgeting app, or spending tracker chart, you can keep a close eye on your expenses. Regularly reviewing and adjusting your spending habits based on your tracking helps you make smarter choices and reach your financial goals. So grab a notebook, download an app, or create a chart and start tracking your spending today. You'll be amazed at how much control you have over your money and how quickly you can reach your goals.

Budgeting for Fun – Saving for Toys and Games

As a kid, I remember wanting a new doll so badly. My parents taught me to set a fun goal to save for it. The first step is to identify what you want to buy. Maybe it's a new game, a cool toy, or even a special trip to the amusement park. Once you know what you want, figure out the total cost. If the doll costs $20, that's your savings target. Knowing the exact amount helps you plan how much to save each week.

Making a budget for fun stuff is the next step! Start by setting aside part of your allowance or money you earn just for this. Maybe you choose to save $2 each week. Set a timeline, too. If you want to buy a toy in ten weeks, you'll need to save every week. Write down your goal and timeline to stay on track. Having a clear plan makes it easier to keep going and stay excited about your goal.

Tracking your savings can be fun! Use a chart to see your progress. Draw sections that show different amounts—each time you save, color in a section. Watching the chart fill up is motivating and makes saving exciting. Celebrate small wins, too! If you want to save $20, celebrate when you reach $5, $10, and $15. You can treat yourself or do something fun. These small celebrations keep you going.

When it's time to buy, think about it carefully. Ask yourself if the item is something you really want and if it's worth the money. The answer you come up with will help you make smart choices and avoid spending on things you don't need. We'll discuss this further in chapter 5.

Setting fun goals for toys or games helps you learn useful money skills. It shows you how to plan, save, and make smart choices. Plus, saving becomes enjoyable, and you feel proud when you reach your goal. So, think about what you really want, set your goal, and start saving. With a bit of planning and patience, you'll be surprised how fast you can reach it!"

Learning from Mistakes – Adjusting Your Budget

Everyone makes mistakes, even with money. Remember when you spent all your allowance on candy and didn't have enough left for the toy you wanted? It happens to everyone. But here's the good news: mistakes are chances to learn. They show us what not to do next time, so instead of feeling bad, see them as a way to get better with money.

One way to spot budgeting mistakes is to keep track of where your money goes. Maybe you've been spending too much on snacks and not enough on saving for that new game. Or maybe you bought something small and forgot to write it down. These little things can add up and mess up your budget.

When you spot a mistake, adjust your budget. If you spent too much on snacks, you could spend less on entertainment that week to cover the extra snack cost. If you forgot to track an expense, add it in to keep your budget accurate.

Preventing future mistakes is about good habits. Set reminders to track your spending, like a note on your phone or a sticky note on your wall. This way, you remember to write down each purchase. Another tip is to review your budget every week. Pick a day to check if you're sticking to your plan and make any changes if needed. This regular check-in helps you catch mistakes early and stay on track.

Fixing mistakes isn't just about the numbers. It's about learning and improving. Each time you make a mistake and fix it, you get better at managing your money. Don't be afraid to mess up! Use those moments to get better. Before long, you'll be great at budgeting.

Making mistakes is part of learning, and even adults mess up with money sometimes. The important thing is to learn from them. By keeping track of your spending, adjusting your budget when needed, and building good habits, you can avoid the same mistakes in the future. And who knows? You might even start helping your parents with their budget!

Family Budgeting – Involving Kids in Household Budgets

Family budgets are like a big map showing how a family manages its money. This map includes all the money the family earns, like salaries or side jobs, and all the money they spend, such as on groceries, bills, and savings. A family budget helps everyone know where the money is going and makes sure there's enough for everything important. It's a plan that helps families avoid spending too much and ensures they have money for things they need.

Ask your parents if they are okay with you learning more about the family budget. You could let them know that getting kids involved in family budgeting has many benefits.

- First, it teaches financial responsibility. When kids like you see how the family's money is managed, you learn that money isn't endless. You understand that every dollar has a purpose. This knowledge helps you make smarter choices with your own money.

- Second, it helps kids like you understand the value of money.

When you see how much things cost, like groceries or electricity, you appreciate the cash you have and spend it more wisely.

Kids can help with simple tasks in the family budget. One fun way is to help review grocery receipts. After a shopping trip, sit down together and look at the receipt. See how much was spent on different items. This activity helps you see where the money goes and how small amounts add up. Another task is suggesting ways to save on family expenses. For example, you can suggest turning off lights when they are not needed to save on electricity. Small actions like these teach kids that even little savings can make a big difference.

Regular family budget meetings are a great way to involve everyone. These meetings can be once a month or whenever it's time to review the budget. During the meeting, the family can discuss financial goals together. Maybe the goal is to save for a family vacation or to buy a new appliance. Talking about these goals helps everyone understand the importance of budgeting. Reviewing the family's budget together lets everyone see what's working and what might need to change. It's a time to celebrate successes and make adjustments if needed.

Family Budget Meeting Agenda

Having a simple agenda can make family budget meetings more effective. Here's an example:

1. **Review last month's budget:** Look at what was earned and spent. See if the budget was followed and discuss any surprises.

2. **Discuss financial goals:** Talk about current goals and any new ones. Update everyone on the progress towards these goals.

3. **Check for savings opportunities:** Brainstorm ways to save

money. Maybe there's a cheaper phone plan or a way to reduce water usage.

4. **Adjust the budget:** If needed, make changes to the budget. Changes could be shifting money from one category to another or setting new savings targets.

Involving kids in these meetings makes them feel like an important part of the family's financial decisions. It gives them a sense of responsibility and helps them learn valuable skills. They see firsthand how planning and teamwork can make a big difference.

Family budgeting can be a team effort. When everyone is involved, the process is more open and educational. Kids learn about money management, the importance of saving, and the value of every dollar. Kids like you gain skills that will help them throughout your life. So, check with your parents, gather around the table, grab those receipts, and start your family budget meeting. It's a great way to for you to learn about money and work together towards common goals.

Chapter 5

Spending Wisely

Imagine this: you're at the toy store, super excited, and the shelves are full of awesome toys everywhere. The coolest action figures, the best board games, the softest stuffed animals—so many choices! But before you grab a toy and run to the checkout, let's talk about spending your money wisely. Spending wisely means making smart choices so you get the most out of your money, like being a detective to find the best deals and avoid wasting cash.

SMART SHOPPING – FINDING THE BEST DEALS

The first step to smart shopping is research. Before you buy something, take some time to learn about it. Read reviews from people who have already bought it. Reviews tell you if a toy breaks easily or if a game is really fun. You can also compare different brands. Maybe one brand's action figure comes with extra accessories or is stronger. Knowing these things helps you make a smart choice.

Sales are a great way to get deals. Look for big sales like back-to-school or Black Friday. During these times, stores give discounts to get more shoppers. Clearance racks are another place to find bargains. Clearance items are usually cheaper because the store needs to make space for new stuff. Keep an eye out for these deals, and you'll save a lot of money.

Shopping online versus in-store each has its ups and downs. Shopping online is super easy because you don't have to leave your house, and there are lots of choices. But you can't see or try the product before buying it. Shopping in-store lets you touch and test the product, which helps you know if it's what you want. But sometimes, in-store shopping doesn't have the same discounts as online. Decide which is more important: the convenience of online shopping or being able to see the product in person.

Making a shopping list is a game-changer. Before you go shopping, write down what you need. This list keeps you focused and helps you avoid buying things you don't need. Put the most important things at the top and stick to the list. It's like having a map to guide you through the store!

Smart Shopping Checklist

Creating a smart shopping checklist can help you get the best deals and avoid impulse buys. Here's a simple checklist for your next shopping trip:

1. **Research the product:** Where is it made? Is it a good product?

2. **Read reviews:** Compare features of different brands.

3. **Look for sales:** Check for seasonal sales (back-to-school, Black

Friday, summer, winter, etc.) Browse clearance racks.

4. **Decide where to shop:** Online for convenience and selection or In-store for seeing and trying products.

5. **Make a shopping list:** Write down everything you need. Prioritize items. Stick to the list.

Using this checklist helps you stay organized and make smart choices. Smart shopping isn't just about finding the best deals; it's about knowing what you're buying and making sure it's worth the money. By researching products, looking for sales, choosing the right place to shop, and making a shopping list, you'll become a smart shopper quickly. So, next time cool toys surround you, remember these tips to shop wisely!

Impulse Buying – How to Avoid It

Impulse buying is when you buy something without planning. You see something cool, and before you know it, you've bought it. The problem is, later, you might wish you hadn't. Maybe you got a toy and realized you didn't really need it. That money could have been saved for something better.

To avoid impulse buying, try to figure out what makes you want to buy things. Sometimes, when you're bored, excited, or even sad, buying something seems like a good idea. But those feelings don't last, and you could end up with stuff you don't need. Stores also make it tempting with bright displays and sale signs.

There are some easy ways to avoid impulse buying.

- One tip is to wait 24 hours before buying something. This gives you time to decide if you really need it. Often, you'll realize you don't. Another tip is to ask if it's a need or a want. Needs are things you have to have, like school supplies. Wants are nice to have, like a new toy. Focus on needs first to make better choices.

- You can also make a wish list. Instead of buying it right away, add it to your list. Later, check the list to see if you still want it. Most times, you might not want it anymore. A wish list is also helpful for birthdays or holidays so others know what you'd like!

Impulse Buying Reflection Exercise

Next time you want to buy something, try this exercise:

1. What is the item?

2. Why do you want it?

3. How do you feel right now (bored, excited, sad)?

4. Is it a need or a want?

5. Can you wait 24 hours before buying it?

After waiting 24 hours, see if you still want it. This will help you think more about your purchases.

Plus, having a wish list makes it easier for parents and grandparents to know what you'd like for birthdays or holidays.

Impulse buying can be tricky to control, but with these strategies, you can make smarter choices.

COMPARING PRICES – MAKING SMART CHOICES

Comparing prices helps you find the best deal. Let's say you want a new video game. One store sells it for $60, but another sells it for $50. If you buy it from the first store without checking, you spend more money than you need to. Comparing prices helps you save so you can keep more money or buy other things.

You can use price comparison websites to compare prices from different stores. You type in the item, and the website shows you where it costs less. If you're at a mall, check different stores and write down the prices. Some stores might have sales that others don't, so it's worth looking around.

It's important to think about the quality of the item, too. Sometimes, cheaper items don't last as long. For example, if you buy a cheap backpack, it might break quickly. A better quality one might cost more but last longer, saving you money over time.

Sometimes, name-brand items are more expensive than generic ones. For example, if a name-brand cereal costs $4 and the generic one costs $2 but tastes the same, why spend extra? This is another way to save.

When you compare prices, think about how long the item will last and whether it's worth the money. Saving money isn't just about spending less now—it's about making sure what you buy will last. This helps you make better choices and keep more of your money.

Comparing prices isn't just for big things. You can do it for everyday items like clothes or snacks. The more you practice, the better you'll get at finding deals. So next time you shop, check prices first to get the best deal and save money!

Using Coupons and Discounts – How to Save Money

Coupons help you save money by giving you discounts on things you buy. You can find coupons in newspapers, online, or in apps. For example, if your favorite snack costs $2, and you have a coupon that makes it $1.50, you save 50 cents. Over time, those savings add up and help you spend less.

Finding coupons can be easy. You can look on coupon websites, use apps, or join store loyalty programs for special discounts. Stores also have sales, and you can use coupons during those sales to save even more.

To use coupons wisely, always check when they expire. Some coupons can only be used for a short time. Combining coupons with sales is a great way to lower prices even more. But remember, don't buy something just because you have a coupon. Only use coupons for things you need.

For example, if your favorite snack is on sale for $2 (instead of $3) and you have a $1-off coupon, you only pay $1. Another example is if a store has a 20% off sale and you have a 10% off coupon. Using both means you save even more.

Coupon and Discount Exercise

Next time you shop, try to find three coupons for things you need. Write down the original price, the price with the coupon, and how much you saved. This will help you see how coupons can save you money.

Saving with Coupons

Item	Original Price	Discounted Price	Savings
Bag of Potato Chips	$ 3.50	$ 2.50	$1.00
Shampoo	$ 5.00	$ 3.50	$1.50
t-shirt	$ 10.00	$ 8.00	$2.00

Using coupons and discounts is a simple way to save. You can find coupons, combine them with sales, and stretch your money further. So, start using your coupons and start saving!

EVALUATING PURCHASES – IS IT WORTH IT?

Before buying something, think about how long it will last and how often you'll use it. For example, if you're getting a new backpack, check if it's made of strong material that can last all year. For things you use every day, like a backpack or shoes, it makes sense to spend a bit more for good quality. But if it's a toy you might only play with a few times, it might not be worth spending a lot on it.

Think about whether the item will actually make your life better. Will you use it a lot, or will it just sit around? For example, a good water bottle that keeps your drink cold all day is something you'll use often. But a toy you only play with once might not be the best use of your money. Make sure it's something you need and will use regularly.

Balancing cost and quality is important. Sometimes, it's better to pay a bit more for something that lasts longer. For example, a well-made pair of shoes costs more but lasts longer than a cheaper pair that wears out quickly. This way, you don't have to keep buying new ones, which saves money over time.

Let's say you need a new school backpack. A cheap one costs $10, and a good one costs $30. The cheap one might seem like a good deal, but if it rips or breaks in a few months, you'll need to buy another one. The better-quality backpack will last longer, so you won't have to spend more money later. The same goes for toys—spending a little more on a strong toy might be better than buying a cheap one that breaks quickly.

Thinking carefully before buying helps you make smart choices. By looking at long-term value, how useful something is, and balancing cost with quality, you can make sure your money is well-spent. This way, you'll get more out of what you buy and enjoy it for longer.

Chapter 6

Investing Basics

One of my grandsons loves collecting baseball cards. He'd trade with friends, always on the lookout for that rare card. One day, his dad said, "You know, some of these cards might be worth more than you bought them for." So, my grandson looked online, and sure enough, some of the cards were worth more than he had paid for them. That's when he got his first taste of investing. It wasn't just about having fun with the cards; it was about thinking ahead and watching his collection grow in value. Investing is a lot like that—it's about putting something aside now with the hope that it will be worth more in the future.

What is Investing? — a Simple Explanation for Kids

Investing means putting your money into something with the expectation that it will grow over time. Think of it like planting a seed. You water it, give it sunlight, and after a while, it turns into a big, beautiful tree. The money you invest is like that seed. You put it in the right place, and it grows, giving you more money later.

People invest their money for several reasons.

1. **To grow their wealth.** If you keep money in a savings account, it doesn't grow very fast. But if you invest it, your money has a chance to grow faster.

2. **To reach their goals.** Investing can help people reach big goals, like buying a car, going to college, or even starting a business. The money they invest now can help them pay for these things later.

3. **To prepare for the future.** By investing, people can have more money when they're older. It's a way to make sure they have enough money later on when they may not want to work as much.

How does investing work?

When you invest, you buy something that you believe will become more valuable over time. There are many things people can invest in, like stocks, bonds, and real estate.

Imagine you buy a comic book for $10. A few years later, that comic book becomes really popular, and now it's worth $50. If you sell it for $50, you make a profit of $40! This is similar to how investing works—you put money into something, and if it becomes more valuable, you can make more money when you sell it.

Different Types of Investments

There are a few types of investments that people use to grow their money, and some are especially interesting for kids. Investing isn't just for grown-ups. Kids can invest, too, and it's a great way to learn about money. Starting small is okay. You don't need a lot of money to begin investing. Even setting aside a little bit each week can add up. Over time, with patience and smart choices, your investments can grow significantly.

But, in order to better understand investing, let's talk about some basic concepts.

Principal is the initial amount of money you invest. It's like a seed you plant.

Return is the profit you make from your investment. It's like the fruit that grows from the seed you planted.

If you invest $100 (the principal)and it grows to $120, your return is $20. The goal is to have a high return, meaning your money grows a lot over time.

 Let's look at some different types of investments-

- **Stocks**

When you buy a stock, you're buying a tiny piece of a company. If the company does well, the value of your stock might go up, and you can sell it for more than you paid. But if the company doesn't do well, the value of your stock might go down. Imagine you decide to invest in a company that makes popular video games. You buy a few shares because you believe the company will continue to create fun and exciting games. As the company grows and makes more games, the value of your shares increases. You can check how your investment is doing by looking at its current value compared to what you paid for it. If the value has gone up, you've made a profit. This is a real-life example of how investing works.

- **Bonds**

Bonds are like loans. When you buy a bond, you're lending money to a company or the government. In return, they pay you back with interest over time. Bonds are usually less risky than stocks, but they also grow slower.

- **Real Estate**

This means buying property, like a house or a piece of land. If the value of the property goes up, you can sell it for more than you paid. People also make money by renting out property.

- **Mutual Funds**

Mutual funds are collections of stocks and bonds that people can buy together. They're like a group project where everyone puts in some money, and the returns are shared. Mutual funds can be a good way to invest because they spread out the risk.

- **Savings Accounts and CDs**

While not technically an "investment," savings accounts and CDs (certificates of deposit)are ways to earn interest on money you save. They're very safe, but the money doesn't grow as fast as other investments. Let's say you put $50 in a savings account that earns 2% interest each year. After one year, you'll have $51. It may not seem like much, but over time, the interest adds up. The more money you save, the more interest you earn. This is a simple and safe way to start investing.

Investing teaches you the importance of planning for the future and making smart financial decisions. It's not just about the money you have now but about growing it for the future. By understanding the basics of investing, you can start making informed choices that will help you reach your financial goals. So, whether it's buying shares in a company or putting money in a savings account, investing is a powerful tool to grow your wealth and achieve your dreams.

RISK AND REWARD

Investing isn't a sure thing. It comes with something called "risk." Risk means there's a chance you could lose money. Different investments have different levels of risk. Some are "low-risk," meaning they're safer but grow slowly. Others are "high-risk," meaning you could make a lot of money or lose some.

Think of it this way: jumping on a trampoline is *low-risk*; you might get a little scared, but you're pretty safe. Skydiving, on the other hand, is *high-risk*. It's a much bigger thrill, but there's more that could go wrong. In investing, low-risk choices are like saving accounts and bonds, while high-risk choices are stocks or real estate.

People invest in things that match their comfort with risk. If they're okay with high risk, they might buy stocks. If they want to play it safe, they might stick with bonds or savings accounts.

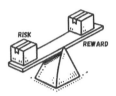

The Power of "Compound Interest" – How Money Grows

Compound interest is one of the most important ideas in investing. It's like magic, but it's actually math! When you earn interest on the money you invest, that interest starts to make its own interest. This is called "compounding."

Here's an example: Imagine you put $100 in an account that earns 10% interest every year. After one year, you have $110. But in the second year, you earn interest on $110, so you end up with $121. This keeps growing faster and faster!

The longer you let your money grow, the bigger it can get, thanks to compounding. This is why starting early is a big advantage.

Compound Interest Growth Chart

This chart shows how your money grows each year. You start with $100 at 5% interest and watch it grow year by year. By the seventh year, you have $140.71. That's an extra $40.71 just from interest. Imagine how much more it could grow if you left it in for 10 or even 20 years!

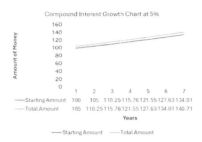

Compound interest teaches you the value of patience and the benefits of saving early. It shows that small, regular investments can grow into something substantial over time. This is why it's important to start saving and investing as soon as possible. The earlier you start, the more time your money has to grow.

So, whether you're saving for a new bike, college, or even a future house, compound interest can help you reach your goals faster. It's like having a magical money tree that keeps growing and producing more money! All you have to do is plant the seed and give it time.

How to Get Started with Investing

If you're excited about investing, here are a few steps to get started.

1. Save Some Money

You don't need a lot to start investing. Even a small amount can grow over time. Maybe you have allowance money or savings from birthdays – that's a good start.

2. Learn the Basics

Reading about investing or asking adults who know about it can help. Understanding terms like "stocks," "bonds," and "risk" will make investing easier.

3. Start Small

You don't need to put all your money into one thing. Try investing a little in something you understand and see how it works.

4. Ask for Help

Talk to your parents or a trusted adult. They can help you choose a safe investment or explain things you don't understand.

5. Be Patient

Investing is a long game. You probably won't see big results right away, but remember – the goal is to grow your money over time.

Setting Goals for Your Money

When you start investing, it's helpful to set goals. A goal gives you something to aim for, like saving up for something special or just watching your money grow. There are two main types of goals in investing:

1. **Short-Term Goals** – These are things you want in the near future, like a new bike or a game console. You might keep money for short-term goals in a savings account because it's safe.

2. **Long-Term Goals** – These are goals you have for the future, like college, a car, or even a trip. Investing is great for long-term goals because you have time to let your money grow.

Tips for Young Investors

- **Invest in What You Know:** If you're interested in a certain company or type of investment, start there. It's easier to understand and follow investments that mean something to you.

- **Track Your Investments:** Keep a notebook or use a simple app to track your investments. This will help you see how your money grows over time.

- **Stay Curious:** The more you learn, the better you'll get. Investing changes over time, and new ideas come up. Staying curious and learning will make you a better investor.

- **Don't Worry About Ups and Downs:** In investing, prices go up and down. Don't worry too much if your investment loses value for a while. Over time, things usually balance out.

Understanding How Stock Markets Work

The stock market is like a big marketplace where people buy and sell stocks. Companies sell shares, or small pieces of ownership, to raise money. When people buy these shares, they own a little part of that company. If the company does well, the value of the shares usually goes up, and people can sell them for a profit.

Stock prices change every day. Sometimes, they go up, and sometimes, they go down. This is normal! Prices change based on how well people think companies will do in the future.

If you buy a stock, remember that you're in it for the long term. The ups and downs don't matter as much as the overall growth over time.

Understanding Dividends

Some companies pay their investors "dividends." Dividends are a way for companies to share some of their profits with people who own their stock. Not all companies pay dividends, but for those that do, it's like getting a small reward for owning their stock.

Why Some People Don't Invest

Not everyone invests, and here's why:

- **Fear of Losing Money:** Some people are afraid of taking risks. They worry about losing money if things don't go well.

- **Lack of Knowledge:** Investing can be confusing, and not everyone takes the time to learn about it.

- **Short-Term Thinking:** Some people want quick results, but investing takes time. They might give up if they don't see quick returns.

Investing takes patience, knowledge, and sometimes a bit of bravery. Learning about it now helps you feel more comfortable and confident when you're ready to start.

Being a Smart Investor

Being a smart investor means making choices that fit your goals and risk level. Here are some ways to be a smart investor:

- **Do Your Homework:** Learn about the investment you're interested in. Know how it works and what risks come with it.

- **Think Long-Term:** Remember, investing is not a get-rich-quick thing. Give your money time to grow.

- **Don't Put All Your Eggs in One Basket:** Try to spread your money across different types of investments. This way, if one doesn't do well, others might still grow.

- **Stay Calm**. The market can be unpredictable. Don't let small price changes worry you. Stick to your plan and trust the process.

The Importance of Starting Young

The best part about learning to invest early is time. When you start young, your money has more time to grow. Even small amounts can add up if you let them grow over many years. Just as with planting a garden, the earlier you plant, the bigger your garden can become.

MAKING MONEY WORK FOR YOU

Investing is all about making your money work for you instead of just sitting around. Money can grow in many ways, and investing gives you the chance to build up money over time.

By now, you have a good idea of what investing is and why it's important. The next steps are about learning more, setting some goals, and taking small steps to start your own investing journey. With time, patience, and a little guidance, you can become a smart investor and make your money grow for your future!

How to Practice Investing Without Real Money

Starting with real money isn't always necessary when you're learning to invest. There are ways to practice investing without spending anything. Here are some ideas:

- **Mock Portfolios:** A mock portfolio is a pretend list of stocks or other investments that you track over time. You can choose a few stocks you're interested in and pretend to "buy" them at their current price. Then, watch how they change over days, weeks, or months. This helps you learn how investments grow and change.

- **Investment Games and Apps:** Some apps and websites let you practice investing with virtual money. You get fake money to buy stocks, bonds, or other investments so you can learn without using real money. These tools are a fun and safe way to learn.

- **Tracking Real Investments:** You can also follow real stocks that interest you and keep track of their performance. For example, if you're interested in a company that makes your favorite video game, see how its stock price changes over time. Write down the prices each day, week, or month and see if you notice any patterns.

By practicing without using real money, you get comfortable with investing and gain confidence before making real financial choices.

Try one of these stock market simulation games to play with your family. Each of you starts with the same amount of fake money. Choose different companies to invest in and track your investments for a month. At the end of the month, see who made the best choices and grew their money the most. Discuss what you learned about investing and what strategies worked best.

Here are a few options:

TheStock Market Game (ages Elementary+)

PIGGYBANK®Fantasy Stock Exchange™ Game for Children - Learn About Stocks & ShareTrading & Win Fab Prizes (ages Middle School and Up)

FreeVirtual Stock Market Simulator Game For Students | TD Bank

These kid-friendly investments teach valuable lessons about money. Savings bonds, savings accounts, and CDs show how money can grow over time. Educational programs like stock market games and investment apps make learning fun and interactive. By starting with these simple investments, you build a strong foundation for future financial success.

The Magic of "Dollar-Cost Averaging"

One method of investing that's great for beginners is called "dollar-cost averaging." It's a fancy term, but the idea is simple: you invest a fixed amount of money regularly, no matter what the stock prices are.

For example, let's say you have $10 each month to invest in a company's stock. If the stock price is low one month, you can buy more shares. If it's high, you buy fewer shares. Over time, this approach helps you buy at an average price and reduces the risk of buying at the wrong time.

Dollar-cost averaging is a great way to get started because:

- You don't have to worry about timing the market.

- You steadily build up your investments.

- It's easier to start with a small amount and stay consistent.

With dollar-cost averaging, the focus is on investing a little each month and letting it add up over time.

Common Mistakes New Investors Make

Investing can be tricky, and beginners sometimes make mistakes. Here's a list of common investing mistakes and tips to avoid them:

1. **Investing Without Research:** It's tempting to jump into investments because they sound exciting, but it's important to learn about them first. Before you invest, make sure you understand what you're buying.

2. **Expecting Quick Gains:** Investing takes time. If you're looking to double your money in a week, it's not the way to go. Be patient, and don't worry if your money doesn't grow right away.

3. **Putting All Money in One Place:** It's risky to invest all your money in one stock or company. If it doesn't do well, you could lose a lot. Spread your money across different investments to stay safe.

4. **Selling Too Quickly When Prices Drop:** Sometimes, people panic and sell when they see the price of their investment go down. But prices go up and down all the time. If you sell too quickly, you might miss the chance for your investment to bounce back.

Learning from these common mistakes can help you become a better investor. Remember, investing is about patience and learning over time.

How to Research Investments

Learning to research investments is an important skill. Here's a simple process for finding out if an investment is a good choice:

1. **Know What the Company Does:** If you're thinking about investing in a company, find out what it makes or does. Do you like the products? Is it a strong company? Understanding the company helps you feel confident in your choice.

2. **Check the Company's Performance:** You can look up how well the company has done in the past. Did its stock price go up or down over the last year? How has it grown over time? Past performance doesn't guarantee future results, but it can give you an idea of the company's success.

3. **Read News and Updates:** Big events, like new products or changes in leadership, can affect a company's stock. Try reading the news to see what's happening with the company.

4. **Compare to Competitors:** Sometimes, it helps to look at other companies in the same industry. If a similar company is doing better, it might be worth considering instead.

Practicing these steps can help you make informed decisions and avoid risky investments.

The Role of Emotions in Investing

Emotions can play a big role in investing, and learning to manage them is important. Here are some emotions that can come up and tips on how to handle them:

1. **Excitement:** When an investment goes up, it's easy to feel excited and want to buy more. But remember to stay calm and stick to your plan. Just because something is going up doesn't mean it will keep going up.

2. **Fear:** If your investment drops, you might feel afraid and want to sell. But remember, prices can bounce back. Selling because of fear can lead to missed opportunities.

3. **Greed:** Sometimes, people get greedy and want to make as much money as possible as quickly as they can. This can lead to risky choices. Investing is best done with patience and balance, not with greed.

4. **Confidence:** Feeling confident is good, but overconfidence can be dangerous. Stick to your research and avoid making quick decisions based only on how you feel.

Managing emotions is one of the hardest parts of investing. Remember to stay calm and stick to your plan, even when prices go up or down.

Understanding Inflation

Inflation is another important concept in investing. Inflation means that prices for things like food, clothes, and toys usually go up over time. This is why items like candy bars might cost more now than they did a few years ago.

Inflation affects investing because if your money doesn't grow faster than inflation, you're actually losing value. For example, if inflation is 2% per year and your money only grows by 1%, you're losing purchasing power.

Investing is a way to try to beat inflation and make sure your money grows faster than prices go up. It's another reason why saving alone isn't enough—investing can help protect your money's value over time.

Long-Term Goals – Planning for Bigger Dreams

Setting long-term money goals is like going on a treasure hunt. You need a clear map to find the treasure at the end! Long-term goals help you save for big things you'll want in the future. Think of saving up for something huge, like college or your first car. These goals take time, but they teach you to save and make smart choices with your money.

Here are some long-term goals that might make sense for you. One is saving for college, which can be super expensive. Starting early makes it easier to afford when the time comes. Another example is saving for a car when you turn 16. Having your own car means freedom, but it costs a lot. Setting a goal to save for it means you'll have the money when you're ready. These goals might feel far away now, but by planning, you can make them happen!

To set long-term goals, first decide what you want to save for and how much money you'll need. For example, if you want to buy a car, find out how much cars cost and set that as your goal. Next, make a timeline. Decide how long you want to save, then break it down into smaller steps. If you want to save $5,000 for a car in five years, figure out how much to save each month. This makes the goal feel doable and keeps you on track.

Keeping track of your progress is super important. Use a goal tracker or a timeline chart to see how much you've saved and how close you are to your goal. This helps you stay motivated. Check your plan often and make changes if you need to. Maybe you can save a bit more, or maybe you need a bit more time. Being flexible keeps you on track.

Goal Tracker Exercise

Make a timeline chart to track your long-term goal. Draw a line with your goal amount at the end. Mark each step along the way, showing how much you need to save each month. Color in each section as you reach your savings milestones. This way, you can see your progress and stay motivated.

Setting long-term goals teaches you patience and planning. Each small step brings you closer to your big dream. Whether you're saving for college, a car, or another big goal, having a plan and tracking your progress makes it possible.

STARTING EARLY — THE BENEFITS OF INVESTING YOUNG

I'm sure many of you have heard the saying, "The early bird catches the worm." I'll bet you thought, "Who wants worms, anyway?" When I first heard that, I thought it was just talking about waking up early. But I came to realize that this is also about the advantages of starting things early, like investing. Starting to invest when you're young gives your money more time to grow. The longer your money sits in an investment, the more it can grow. This happens because of the magic of compound interest, which we talked about earlier. The longer your money is invested, the more interest it earns, and the more your investment grows.

Investing early also helps build good financial habits. When you start young, you get used to the idea of saving and investing regularly. It becomes a normal part of your routine. You learn to set aside a portion of your allowance or earnings and invest it. This habit sticks with you as you grow older, making it easier to manage your money wisely. Early investing teaches you the importance of financial planning. You start to see the benefits of thinking ahead and making smart choices with your money. It's like learning to brush your teeth every day. It becomes a habit that keeps you healthy in the long run.

Let's look at some real-life examples of young investors who started early and reaped the benefits.

Mikaila Ulmer was just four years old when she got stung by bees twice in one week. Instead of being scared, she became fascinated by bees and their role in the environment. With her parents' help, she started a lemonade business using her grandmother's recipe and sweetened it with honey. She called it "Me & the Bees Lemonade." By the time she was 11, her lemonade was sold in stores across the country. After 10 years in business, Mikaila's company has become a national brand. Mikaila's story shows how starting early and following your passion can lead to amazing success.

Evan started a YouTube channel called "EvanTubeHD" when he was just eight years old. ((2) Faceboo. He made videos about toys and games, and his channel quickly became popular. As his channel grew, Evan and his parents decided to invest the money he earned from YouTube. They set up a savings account and invested in stocks. By starting early, Evan learned the value of investing and watched his money grow over time. His early start gave him a head start in building wealth for the future.

Brennan Agranoff became a CEO at the age of 13. After noticing all that of his classmates were wearing plain white athletic socks at a basketball game, Agranoff wondered whether he could start a new craze by making socks with custom designs. He launched his online-only business, **Hoop-Swagg**, in 2013, and it's since taken off in a big way.

Being consistent is super important for investing. Regularly putting money in your savings or investment accounts helps your money grow, like watering a plant every day. If you water it daily, it grows strong. But if you forget, it starts to droop. Setting up automatic transfers to your investment account makes sure you don't forget to invest. Even small amounts can add up over time and make a big difference.

To help you stay on track, try setting up a simple system. Each week, save a bit from your allowance or chores money. You can start with something small, like $2 or $5. The main thing is to keep doing it every week. You could also ask your parents to set up automatic transfers from your savings account to your investment account so your money is invested without you having to remember.

Starting early and being consistent with your investments teaches you about patience and planning ahead. You'll see how even small, regular investments can grow over time like a tree getting taller and stronger each year. The earlier you start, the more time your money has to grow, and the bigger your "money tree" will be.

Investing young helps you make smart money choices for life. It helps you build wealth, reach your goals, and enjoy the benefits of financial security. So, start today. Plant the seeds for your financial future and watch them grow!

Chapter 7

Generosity and Charity

W hen my daughters were little, I remember that our neighbor, Mrs. Thompson, slipped on the ice and hurt her leg. She couldn't get out to buy groceries, so my daughters and I decided to help. We bundled up, went to the store, and got everything she needed. When we brought the groceries to her, she was so happy she had tears in her eyes. That moment made all of us feel warm and joyful inside, even though it was freezing outside. My daughters told me they learned that helping others made them feel good and filled their hearts with happiness.

WHY BE GENEROUS? – THE JOY OF GIVING

Giving to others can make you feel truly happy. When you help someone, you get a warm, fuzzy feeling inside. It's like eating your favorite ice cream on a hot day. This feeling happens because doing good for others releases chemicals in your brain that make you feel good. It's science! Helping others also boosts your self-esteem. When you see the difference you've made in someone's life, you feel proud and confident. Acts of kindness build our self-worth and make us realize how powerful our actions can be.

Generosity can create positive changes in the world. Imagine you donate your old toys to a children's hospital. Those toys can make a sick child's day brighter. It's like bringing sunshine on a cloudy day. Helping others can also improve your community. When you help a neighbor with their groceries or clean up a park, you make your community a better place to live. Your small acts of kindness can ripple out and inspire others to do the same, creating a wave of positivity.

The Story of Jessica.

Real-life examples of generosity can be truly inspiring. Take the story of a child who raised money for a friend in need. Jessica, an eight-year-old girl, found out her friend needed a wheelchair. She decided to help by baking cookies and selling them. Jessica worked hard, and with the help of her family and friends, she raised enough money to buy the wheelchair. Her friend was overwhelmed with joy. Jessica's act of kindness not only helped her friend but also showed everyone how one person can make a big difference.

Friends of the Johnson Family

Another heartwarming story is about a community coming together to support a family. The Johnsons lost their home in a fire. They had nowhere to go and lost everything. But their neighbors didn't let them face it alone. Everyone pitched in to help. Some donated clothes and food, while others offered a place to stay. They even organized a fundraiser to help the Johnsons rebuild their home. The community's generosity brought hope and comfort to the Johnsons during a tough time. It showed how love and kindness can turn a tragedy into a story of hope.

Reflection Section: Acts of Kindness

Think about a time when someone did something kind for you.

How did it make you feel? Write or draw about it in a journal.

Now, think of a way you can do something kind for someone else this week. It could be helping a friend with homework, sharing your favorite book, or even just giving a compliment.

Write or draw about your plan and how you think it will make the other person feel.

Giving is more than just helping others. It's about feeling good inside and making the world a better place. When you give, you create a ripple effect of kindness. Your actions inspire others, and together, you can make a big impact. So, the next time you see someone in need, remember that your small act of kindness can brighten their day and fill your heart with joy.

WAYS TO GIVE – TIME, MONEY, AND TALENTS

Giving doesn't always mean handing over money. Sometimes, the best way to help is by giving your time. Kids can make a big difference by volunteering at local events. Think about helping at a community fair or a school fundraiser. Even simple tasks like handing out flyers or helping to set up booths can be a big help. Another great way to give your time is by spending it with elderly neighbors. Many older folks feel lonely and would love some company. You could visit them, play games, or even read a book together. Your presence can brighten their day and make them feel cared for.

Donating money is a great way to help others. Even if you don't have a lot, every bit counts. You could start by saving a small part of your allowance to donate. This helps you get used to giving and saving for a good cause. You can also join fundraisers. Schools and communities often have events to raise money, like bake sales, car washes, or fun runs. These events help raise money and bring people together.

Everyone has unique talents that can help others. If you play an instrument or love art, you could perform at a community center or paint something nice for a local park. Imagine playing music at a senior center or painting a mural in your neighborhood. Your talent can bring happiness to others! If you're good at schoolwork, you could help younger kids with their homework. Tutoring a friend or sibling can make a big difference for them and can help you practice, too.

Combining different ways to give back can have a bigger impact. For example, you could organize a bake sale and then donate the money you raise to a local shelter. That way, you're using your time, effort, and money to help people in need. Another idea is volunteering at an animal shelter and bringing supplies like pet food, blankets, or toys. You could ask friends and family to donate items and then deliver them to the shelter. Combining your efforts shows how teamwork can make a big difference!

Interactive Exercise: Plan Your Giving

Think about how you want to give back. Make a plan by answering these questions:

1. How can you give of your time? List two activities you can do to help others.

2. How much of your allowance can you save for donations? Write down an amount.

3. What talents do you have? List one way you can use your talent to help someone.

4. How can you combine your efforts with others? Plan a small project, like a bake sale or a supply drive.

Giving comes in many forms. Whether you're volunteering your time, donating money, or sharing your talents, each act of kindness makes a difference. Your efforts, big or small, can create a ripple effect of positivity in your community. So, think about what you can do, make a plan, and start giving back. Your actions can inspire others and bring joy to those in need.

Choosing a Charity – Finding Causes You Care About and The Importance of Giving Back

Investing can help you make more money, but it's also important to think about how you can help others. Many successful investors choose to give back to their communities or support causes they care about.

Giving back doesn't just mean donating money; it can also mean sharing what you've learned. As you grow and learn more about investing, you might choose to help others start their own investing journeys. Whether you donate, teach, or volunteer, giving back is a great way to make a difference.

Finding a cause you care about makes giving even more special. Start by thinking about what interests you. Do you love animals? Care about the environment? Want to help other kids learn? Health is another big area where charities work. Think about what excites you. Is it helping a cute puppy find a home or cleaning up a park? When you find something you're passionate about, supporting it feels more exciting.

Next, decide if you want to help locally or globally. Local causes are close to home, like helping an animal shelter, a food bank, or a community garden in your neighborhood. You can see the difference you're making nearby. Global causes help people or animals far away, like providing clean water in Africa or saving animals in the Amazon. Both are important—choose what feels right for you.

Once you know what you're interested in, it's time to search for charities. Not all charities are the same. Some use donations well, and others don't. Look up charity ratings on sites like Charity Navigator or GuideStar to find ones that use their money wisely. Read about what the charity does and how it helps. This way, you know your money will make a real difference.

Getting your family involved can make it even better. Have a family chat about different charities. Share what you find and listen to what your family thinks. Together, you can pick a charity that everyone feels good about. It's a great way to work toward a goal together and teach younger siblings about helping others, too.

Having a personal connection to a cause can make it even more meaningful. If you or someone you know has dealt with something like cancer, supporting a cancer research charity feels personal. Even if you don't have a direct connection, choose a cause that matches your values. If you believe in education for all, supporting a charity that builds schools can feel very fulfilling.

Activity: Family Charity Research

Gather your family for a charity research session. Use a computer or tablet to look up different charities. Check their ratings and read about their missions. Discuss what you find and make a list of top choices. Here are some websites to get you started:

- Charity   Navigator https://www.charitynavigator.org/

- GuideStar   https://www.guidestar.org/

- GreatNonprofits   https://greatnonprofits.org/reviews/

Choosing a charity to support is a thoughtful process. By identifying your interests, researching charities, involving your family, and finding a personal connection, you make sure your donations go to a good cause. It's not just about giving money. It's about making a real difference in something you care about. So, take your time, do your homework, and choose a charity that excites you. You'll feel great knowing your support is making the world a better place.

MAKING DONATIONS – HOW TO GIVE MONEY WISELY

Giving money to help others is a wonderful way to make a difference. But just like with your own spending, it's smart to have a plan. The following are a few ways for you to plan.

- One way to start is to set a donation budget.

Think about how much of your allowance or earnings you want to give. A good rule of thumb is to choose a percentage. For example, you might decide to donate 10% of whatever money you get. If you earn $10 a week, you set aside $1 for donations. This way, you always know how much you're giving, and it becomes a regular habit.

·   Another way is to keep a donation jar.

Grab an empty jar and label it "Donations." Every time you get your allowance or earn some money, put your donation amount into the jar. Watching the jar fill up is exciting and reminds you of the good you're doing. When the jar is full, you can decide where to donate the money.

When donating, safety is super important. Always donate through official charity websites. These sites are safe, so make sure your money goes to the right place. Don't give cash to strangers or places that seem sketchy. If you're unsure, ask a parent or adult to help check if the charity is real. This way, you know your donation will be used properly.

Knowing how your donation is used can make it feel even more special. Charities use money for different things. Some fund specific projects, like building a playground or buying books for a library. Others give direct help, like food for people in need or medical care. Knowing how your money helps can make you feel proud, as if you're part of a team that is making the world better.

Keeping track of your donations is a good habit. Use a donation log to write down each time you give money. Include the date, amount, and charity name. This lets you see all the good you've done and makes it easy to remember your contributions. You can look back and feel proud of the impact you've made. Plus, it helps you stay organized and reach your donation goals!

Donation Log Template

Here's a simple template you can use for your donation log:

Donation Log

Date	Amount	Charity	Notes
Jan. 5	$5	Local Animal Shelter	helped buy food for the animals
Feb. 10	$10	Children's Hospital	contributed to new toys fund
Mar. 15	$4	Community Food Bank	provided meals for families

You can use a log like this to help you stay on top of your donations and see the difference you're making over time.

Making donations is a powerful way to give back. By setting a budget, maintaining a donation jar, and practicing safe donation habits, you can ensure your money goes to good causes. Understanding how charities use your donations and keeping track of your contributions makes the experience even more rewarding. So, grab a jar, set your budget, and start making a difference today.

VOLUNTEERING – GIVING YOUR TIME

Volunteering is an amazing way to give back to your community and build new skills. When you volunteer, you get to learn new things and gain experience. Maybe you'll learn how to organize an event or how to work as part of a team. These skills are handy now and will be super useful when you're older. Plus, volunteering often involves meeting new people. You can make friends who share your interests and passions. These connections can last a lifetime and make your community feel more like home.

Finding the right volunteer opportunities can be as simple as looking around your neighborhood. Local community centers and libraries often need volunteers for events and programs. They might need help setting up for a book fair or organizing a summer reading program. Schools and church groups are also great places to start. They usually have ongoing projects that need extra hands. Ask your teachers or group leaders if they know of any volunteer opportunities. They'll be thrilled to have you help out.

Before you start volunteering, it's important to prepare. First, understand the responsibilities of the role. If you're helping at a community clean-up, know what tasks you'll be doing, like picking up trash or planting flowers. Make sure you get the necessary permissions. If you're under 18, you'll likely need your parents' permission to volunteer. Some places might also require training. For example, if you're reading to younger kids at the library, they might train you on how to engage the children and read aloud effectively. Being prepared ensures you can do your best and enjoy the experience.

Volunteering can make a huge difference in your community. One great example is reading to younger children at the library. You can help them discover the joy of books and improve their reading skills. You might even become their role model. Another impactful activity is participating in community clean-up events. These events help keep your neighborhood clean and beautiful. You get to spend time outdoors, work with others, and see the immediate results of your efforts. It's rewarding to know that your hard work is making your community a better place.

Volunteering is like a superpower. It helps you grow, meet new people, and make a positive impact. Whether you're organizing books at the library, planting trees in the park, or helping at a local event, your time and effort make a difference. So, look around, find an opportunity that excites you, and start volunteering. You'll gain more than you give and make your community shine.

Family Giving – Making Generosity a Family Activity

Creating family-giving traditions is a fantastic way to bond and make a difference together. Imagine setting aside a day each year for a family charity event or fundraiser. You could participate in a local charity walk or run together, raising money for a cause you all care about. Maybe you plan an annual family volunteer day where you spend time helping at a food bank or animal shelter. These traditions become special family memories, and they also show kids the importance of giving as a lifelong practice.

Collaborative projects can be a lot of fun and very rewarding. Why not come together as a family to create care packages for people in need? Gather items like toiletries, snacks, and warm socks, then assemble the packages and deliver them to a local shelter. Another idea is organizing a family garage sale. Collect items you no longer need, from clothes to toys, and sell them. Use the money you raise to donate to a charity or fund a community project. Working together on these projects not only helps others but also strengthens family bonds.

Let your parents know that you would like to know more about generosity. One simple way is by talking about it during family meals. Discuss why giving is important and how it helps others. Share stories of people who have made a difference through acts of kindness. Involve kids in making donation decisions. Let them choose a charity to support or decide how to set aside a portion of the family budget for giving. These discussions help kids understand the impact of their actions and the value of generosity.

Celebrating acts of generosity within the family can be very motivating. You could create family recognition awards for acts of kindness. Maybe someone gets a "Helper of the Month" certificate for going above and beyond to help others. Share stories of impact and success at family gatherings. Talk about how your donations or volunteer work have made a difference. Celebrate these achievements with a special meal or a fun family outing. Recognizing and celebrating generosity reinforces its importance and encourages everyone to keep giving.

Let's make it a habit to share with others. Helping others boosts your self-esteem. When you see the difference you've made in someone's life, you feel proud and confident. Acts of kindness build our self-worth and make us realize how powerful our actions can be.

Generosity can create positive changes in the world, and your small acts of kindness can ripple out and inspire others to do the same, creating a wave of positivity.

Chapter 8

Protecting Your Money

Here's a story about the time my friend Susan got tricked into buying a "magical" pet rock online. She was so excited, thinking it would glow in the dark and maybe even sing! She saved up her allowance and sent her money off, only to receive a plain old rock from the backyard. She was heartbroken, and even worse, she was out of her hard-earned cash. That's when we both learned a valuable lesson about protecting our money from scams.

WHAT IS A SCAM? – RECOGNIZING FRAUD

So, what exactly is a scam? A scam is a dishonest scheme designed to trick people into giving away their money or personal information. Scammers are sneaky and clever. They come up with all sorts of ways to fool you. They might promise amazing prizes or claim you owe money for something you never bought. Their goal is to trick you into handing over your money or personal info.

One type of scam you might come across is an online scam. Imagine you're playing your favorite game, and a pop-up ad promises you free game currency if you click on a link. Sounds too good to be true, right? That's because it is. Clicking that link could lead to a fake website designed to steal your personal details or even install harmful software on your device. Another common online scam is fake contests. You might get an email saying you've won a big prize, but to claim it, you need to pay a fee or provide personal information. Legitimate contests never ask for money upfront.

Phone scams are another sneaky trick. You might get a call from someone pretending to be a bank or a tech support agent. They might say there's a problem with your account and ask for your password or credit card number. Remember, real banks never ask for your personal info over the phone. Always hang up and call your bank directly if you're unsure.

In-person scams happen in real life. Has someone come to your door selling candy for a school fundraiser? They might look and sound convincing, but they could be pocketing the cash instead of supporting the school. Always check with your parents before buying anything from door-to-door sellers.

Recognizing warning signs can help you avoid scams. One big warning sign is when someone offers you something out of the blue, like an email or call saying you won a prize or a great deal. If you didn't enter the contest, you probably didn't win anything! Another warning sign is if someone asks for personal information, like your address, phone number, or bank info. Be careful if they push you to hurry up and decide. Scammers do this to make you feel rushed so you make quick decisions. And remember, if an offer sounds way too good, it probably isn't real.

Let's look at some examples to make this easier to understand.

- You get an email saying you've won a big prize. The email tells you to click a link and enter your personal details to claim it.

Do you claim it?   YES or NO.

The answer is NO. This is a common trick called phishing. The link might go to a fake

- You get an email from a "bank" saying there's a problem with your account and asking you to confirm your details.

Do you reply to the email with your information? YES or NO.

The answer is NO. Real banks don't ask for information like this by email. If you get a message like that, tell your parents, and they can help you contact your bank directly.

- You get a flattering message or tempting ad to pay an entry fee to join a talent contest or casting call.

Do you reply to the message? YES or NO.

The correct answer is NO. In addition to stealing your money, scammers may also steal your personal information or end up with photos or videos of you. Talk to your parents about this right away.

Scam Safety Checklist

1. **Verify the Source:** Check if the message or call is from a trusted source.

2. **Don't Share Personal Info:** Never give out personal information unless you're sure it's safe.

3. **Look for Red Flags:** Be wary of unsolicited offers, requests for personal information, and deals that seem too good to be true.

4. **Ask an Adult:** If you're unsure, always ask a parent or trusted adult for advice.

5. **Report Scams:** If you encounter a scam, have your parents report it to the proper authorities like the Federal Trade Commission (FTC).

Understanding scams and knowing how to recognize them can save you from losing your money or personal information. Stay alert, trust your instincts, and always double-check before sharing your details. And next time someone offers you a magical pet rock, remember Sarah's story and think twice!

Quick Review of Common Scams for Kids – What to Look out for

Online gaming is a lot of fun, but there are scammers who try to trick you. One common scam is fake in-game purchases. You might see an ad for a new skin or weapon for a super low price. You click it and pay, but you never get the item. The scammer just takes your money. Another trick is offering free coins. They might message you saying you can get coins if you share your login info. Don't do it—they're just trying to steal your account.

Social media is also a place where scammers try to fool people. You might get a friend request from someone you don't know. They might act friendly, then start asking for money, saying they're in trouble. It's a scam. Another trick is links to fake websites. You might see a post or message with a link promising free concert tickets or discounts on toys. These links can lead to fake sites designed to steal your info. Be careful with links from people you don't know.

Emails and texts can be scams, too. You might get an email that looks like it's from your bank asking you to change your password. This is a phishing email. It looks real, but it's fake, and the link leads to a site that steals your password. Texts can be scams, too. You might get a text saying you've won a prize and need to click a link or share your info. These messages might look like they're from real places, but they're not. Always double-check, and don't share your info.

Watch out for school-related scams, too. You might hear about a school fundraiser, like selling candy or raffle tickets. Scammers could set up fake fundraisers to keep the money for themselves. Another trick is fake deals on school supplies or tickets to school events. You might get an email or flyer with a special offer that asks for money upfront, but the supplies don't exist. Always check with your teachers or school office before getting involved in any fundraiser or special deal.

Scam Safety Exercise

Write down three types of scams you've learned about. Share them with your family and talk about ways to avoid them. This will help you remember and stay safe from scammers.

Scam 1:

Scam 2:

Scam 3:

By knowing about these common scams, you can protect yourself and your money. Understanding how scammers operate helps you recognize their tricks and avoid falling for them. Stay alert, trust your instincts, and always verify before sharing any personal information or money. And remember, if something seems too good to be true, it probably is!

PROTECTING PERSONAL INFORMATION – STAYING SAFE ONLINE

Think of your personal information like a secret treasure chest you need to protect. Personal information includes things like your name, address, phone number, birthday, and Social Security number. This info is unique to you, almost like your secret identity. If someone else gets this information, they can pretend to be you, which can cause big problems.

Keeping this information private is super important. First, it stops identity theft. Identity theft is when someone steals your info and uses it to act like they're you. They might open bank accounts, get credit cards, or do bad things in your name. This can mess up your money and take forever to fix. Also, keeping your info private stops people from getting into your accounts. If someone has your info, they might hack your email or social media, which can lead to even more trouble.

There are ways to protect your info online. Only share it with trusted websites. Check if a website has "https" in its link—the"s" means it's secure. Use strong passwords for your accounts with a mix of letters, numbers, and symbols. Never share your passwords with anyone except your parents, and change them regularly to stay safe.

If something seems too good to be true, it probably is!

To stay safe online, log out of accounts when you're done, especially if you're on a shared computer. This stops others from getting into your accounts. Also, don't click on strange links. If you get a link from someone you don't know, ignore it. These links can lead to fake sites that steal your info or put bad stuff on your device.

Imagine you're at school and using a computer in the library. After checking your email, log out completely before leaving so the next person can't get into your account. Or, say you get a message from a stranger with a link to a "free gift." Instead of clicking, delete the message and tell your parents.

Your personal information is valuable; guard it carefully. By knowing what info is personal and taking simple steps to protect it, you can keep your online experiences safe and fun.

Safe Online Shopping – Tips for Kids

Online shopping can be a lot of fun. You can find almost anything you want, like new toys or cool gadgets. But to shop safely, you need to know how to keep your money and personal information safe. First, check if the website is secure. Look at the URL—if it starts with "https," the "s" means it's secure, like a safety badge that shows your information is protected. Also, check for safe ways to pay, like PayPal or credit card options. These add extra protection to make sure your money goes to the right place.

Watch out for fake websites, too. Scammers make fake sites that look real but just want to steal your money or info. One way to spot fake websites is to check their addresses carefully. A small difference in spelling can mean it's a scam. It also helps to read reviews. If lots of people say bad things about the site, or if there are no reviews, it's best to avoid it. Real sites usually have plenty of reviews from other buyers.

Always involve your parents in online shopping. They can help you check if a site is real and if a product is worth it. Before buying, ask them to go over the site with you and talk about how much you plan to spend. This way, you'll get better at handling your money and learn to avoid spending too much. Plus, it can be fun to shop together and learn how to make smart choices.

Let's go through an example of safe online shopping. Say you find a toy you really want. You check the URL and see it has "https," so it's secure. Next, you check the payment options, and they accept PayPal, which is a safe choice. Then, you read some reviews and see people are happy with their purchases. Now, it's time to ask your parents for help. You show them the website, and they help you set up a PayPal account to make the purchase. You finish the order, get a confirmation email, and everything is secure!

Or imagine you're looking for a new book. You find it on a website you don't know about. So, you look up the website name and "reviews." You find mixed reviews—some people liked it, others had issues with shipping. To be safe, you decide to look for the book on a more trusted website with better reviews. This way, you avoid any problems and get your book without hassle.

Safe online shopping is all about being careful. By choosing secure websites, avoiding fake ones, and getting help from your parents, you can keep your money and info safe. Look for "https" in the URL, check for safe payment options, and read reviews. With these tips, you'll be able to enjoy online shopping while staying safe and secure.

TALKING ABOUT MONEY – OPEN CONVERSATIONS WITH FAMILY

Talking about money with your family might feel weird at first, but it's super important. It helps everyone understand each other better. When you talk openly about money, you learn from each other's experiences. For example, your grandparents might share stories about saving up for their first house, and your parents could explain how they budget for monthly bills. These talks can help you get better at managing your own money.

One cool thing to talk about is budgeting and saving. Ask your family how they decide what to spend and what to save. You might pick up some useful tricks, like using a shopping list to avoid buying things you don't need. Another good topic is avoiding scams. Your parents can tell you about scams they've seen and how they protect themselves. This can help you avoid scams and keep your money safe.

It's important to create a safe space to talk about money. Be open with your family about any money questions you have. Encourage everyone to ask questions so no one feels embarrassed. You could even start a weekly money chat where everyone can share their thoughts. This keeps everyone on the same page and makes talking about money easier.

Here are some examples of family money talks.

- Imagine your family is planning a vacation. You could all sit down and plan the budget together. Talk about how much money you have saved and how much you'll need for travel, food, and fun stuff. This helps everyone understand the costs and makes planning more exciting.

- Another example is talking about goals. Maybe you're saving for a new bike, and your parents are saving for a new car. Chat about how you can all save a little each week to reach your goals. This helps you see that everyone's working towards something and shows you the value of saving.

These talks show that money isn't just about spending—it's about making smart choices, setting goals, and working together as a family. You'll learn that everyone has different tips and advice. So, next time you're around the dinner table, bring up a money topic. You might be surprised by how much you learn and how fun it can be to talk about money with your family.

FINANCIAL GOALS – SETTING AND ACHIEVING YOUR OWN GOALS

Setting money goals is like planning a big adventure! You need a clear destination and a map to get there.

Let's start with short-term goals. These are things you want soon, like saving for a cool new toy or a fun outing. Think of something you want in the next few weeks or months, write it down, and check how much it costs. This is your target. Once you know your goal, break it down into smaller steps, like saving a few dollars each week from your allowance.

Now, let's talk about long-term goals. These are bigger dreams that take longer, like saving for college or a car. They might seem far away, but starting early makes it easier. Let's say you want to save for college. Even if you don't know the exact amount, try to get a rough idea. Then, figure out how many years you have to save and break down the total amount by year. Breaking big goals into smaller steps makes them easier to handle.

Step-by-step plan to reach your goals

1. Pick your goal and the amount you need.

Let's say you want a new bike that costs $200—that's your goal.

2. Create a savings plan. Decide how much to save each week or month.

If you save $10 each week, you'll reach your goal in 20 weeks.

3.   Write down your plan and stick to it.

It might help to put a picture of the bike where you can see it every day to stay motivated.

4.   Track your progress. Use a goal tracker or savings chart to make it fun.

Draw a chart with your goal at the top and mark each step as you save money.

Color in each section as you get closer to your goal. It shows you how close you are and keeps you excited.

Review your plan regularly and adjust if needed. Maybe you can save extra money for a few weeks or find new ways to earn money.

Stay flexible and keep going!

5.   Celebrate your progress

When you hit a milestone, treat yourself with something small, like a favorite snack or fun activity.

Share your progress with family and friends—they'll cheer you on and help you stay motivated.

Celebrating each step makes the journey more fun and keeps you focused on your goal.

Setting and achieving money goals teaches you important skills like planning, patience, and sticking with them. Your goals might start small, like saving for a toy, but these skills will help you reach even bigger goals later on. Keep setting new goals and enjoy reaching them. Whether it's a toy, a bike, or even saving for college, each goal is a step toward a bright future.

Chapter 9

Interactive Learning and Family Activities

What are some of your family's traditions? When our kids were about your age, we'd gather around the kitchen table every Sunday evening for "Family Fun Night." Sometimes, we played board games; other times, we baked cookies. But our kids liked it best when we did quizzes. We would come up with all sorts of questions and compete to see who could answer the most. It was always a blast; little did we know everyone was learning something. That's the magic of quizzes—they make learning fun!

FUN FINANCIAL QUIZZES

Quizzes are a fantastic way to test what you know about money. They're not just for school; you can make them part of your family-fun time. Imagine sitting around the table, each with a quiz sheet in hand. The questions can range from simple to tricky, making everyone think and learn. Financial quizzes can include multiple-choice, true or false questions and matching terms with definitions. They cover many topics, so there's something for everyone.

Here are some sample questions. These will give you an idea of what to expect and how much fun it can be.

- To start, think about this question: "What is a budget?"

You could have multiple-choice answers like:

A) A plan for spending money,

B) A type of cookie,

C) A new video game.

- Here's another one: "What are needs vs. Wants?"

You could make this a true or false question:

"True or False: Needs are things you must have to live, and wants are things that are nice to have."

- For something a bit more advanced: "How does compound interest work?"

A matching term question might be: "Match the term with its definition:"

Match the Term with its Definition

terms	definitions
Principal	Earning money on both the initial amount and the interest
Interest	The initial amount of money invested
Compound Interest	The profit made from investing

Taking quizzes with your family isn't just about getting the right answers — it's about working together and learning cool stuff along the way. When a tough question pops up, you can share ideas and figure out the answer as a team. It's like solving a fun puzzle together!

And let's be real — a little friendly competition makes things even better. Who doesn't love a good challenge to see who knows the most (or who can come up with the funniest answer)? So grab some snacks, pick a quiz, and let the family fun begin!

If you're looking to make your own quizzes, there are plenty of resources to help. Online quiz platforms are a great place to start. Here are a few.

Goalsetter (*Goalsetter- Education First Family Finance*)

- *Goalsetter is a platform that combines a debit card for kids and teens, financial education quizzes and videos, and investing features.*

- *Learn how to save, invest, spend, and earn with goalsetter's award-winning **app** and curriculum.*

Greenlight

- ***Features**: Greenlight offers a debit card and banking app for kids and teens. It provides parental controls, automated savings goals, and investing options.*

- ***Financial Education**: The app includes educational resources, quizzes, and lessons to help kids and teens understand personal finance.*

- *Investing: With parental approval, kids can invest in stocks and ETFs, giving them hands-on experience managing investments.*

BusyKid

- **Features**: *BusyKid combines a chore management system with a prepaid debit card. Kids can earn an allowance, save money, and spend using their BusyKid Visa card.*

- **Financial Education**: *Through interactive tools and quizzes, kids learn how to manage their earnings and budget for the future.*

- **Investing**: *BusyKid allows users to invest in stocks and offers lessons on how investments work.*

Quizzes are an awesome way to learn. They help you remember what you've learned, figure out where you need more practice, and make learning fun. So grab some paper, call your family, and get ready for some money quiz action. You might be surprised by how much you learn — and how much fun you have!

GAMES MAKE MONEY SKILLS FUN!

Who knew playing games could help you learn how to handle money? Classic games like *Monopoly* and *The Game of Life* are awesome for teaching money smarts while you play.

In *Monopoly*, you get to buy properties like Boardwalk and charge rent when other players land there. The goal? Earn money and avoid going broke! You'll learn about spending wisely and making smart investments.

In *The Game of Life*, you move through life events like getting a job, buying a house, and starting a family. You make choices about saving money, paying off loans, and even what job to take. It's all about planning ahead and managing your cash.

These games sneak in money lessons about earning (money coming in) and spending (money going out). *Monopoly* shows how investing works — buy properties, collect rent, and build houses or hotels to make more cash. *The Game of Life* shows how decisions like going to college or picking a high-paying job can impact your money — sometimes you earn more but have bigger expenses too.

Online money games are super fun too! In *Hot Shot Business*, you run a business and make decisions about advertising, products, and hiring employees. Your choices affect your profits, teaching you about budgeting and running a company.

Want action? Try *Financial Football*, where you answer money questions to move down the field and score touchdowns. It's sports meets money smarts!

Playing money games is a fun way to learn important skills like saving, investing, and budgeting — all while having a blast. So grab your family, set up a game night, and get ready for some money-savvy fun. You'll be surprised how much you can learn — and how much fun you'll have!

FAMILY BUDGETING CAN BE FUN!

Who says talking about money has to be boring? Imagine sitting down with your family, snacks in hand, paper and pens ready, planning fun stuff while making sure all the important things are covered. Having a family budget meeting once a month can actually be pretty cool! It's a time for everyone to chat about money, set goals, and work together as a team.

Everyone in the family can pitch in! Little kids can collect and sort receipts, while older kids might help with the math. Parents keep track of everything and make sure it's right. Working together like this shows that managing money isn't just about paying bills — it's about saving up for fun trips, cool gadgets, and things everyone needs.

Why is family budgeting awesome?

1. **Learn Good Money Habits:** When you know what your family is saving for, you'll think twice before asking for extra stuff.

2. **Teamwork Rules:** Budgeting helps everyone understand each other's needs. Maybe your sibling wants a new bike while you're saving for a gaming console.

3. **No Surprises:** Everyone knows where the money's going, so there's no "Wait, we can't afford that?!" moments.

Here are some simple family budgeting activities to try.

Let's say you're planning a family vacation. With your family-

1. Start by picking a destination.

2. Work together to list the costs for travel, staying, food, and fun activities.

3. Get these expenses written down and decide how much to save each month.

Each family member can even pitch in by saving a bit of their allowance. It's a great way to learn the value of saving for something everyone can enjoy.

For holiday spending, get with your family-

1. List expected costs for gifts, food, and decorations.

2. Set a total budget and stick to it.

3.   Involve kids by letting them help plan and shop.

This teaches you to make smart choices with money.

To make budgeting more fun, try using charts or apps we've learned about to track income and spending. You can even set up a savings jar for specific goals. Every time you add money to the jar, you're closer to reaching your goal, and everyone stays motivated.

Patience Reward Chart

Creating a patience reward chart can help you stay motivated to wait before spending. Here's a simple example:

Patience Reward Chart	
Days waited	Reward
3	small treat
7	extra 15 minutes of screen time
10	favorite treat
14	extra 30 minutes of screen time
21	small toy or game
30	special outing with family

Remember, delayed gratification (waiting to get something you want) is an important idea. It's about being patient and making smart choices, even when it's tempting to take a reward right away. By being patient now, you learn to make thoughtful decisions and can better appreciate the value of your hard-earned money.

Chapter 10

Conclusion

O kay, young saver and future money master- We are about to wrap up this journey. But, before we do, let's talk about why knowing about money is so important. Understanding money helps you make smart choices. It sets you up for success. Imagine being able to save for something you really want or knowing how to avoid scams.

Now, here's a little challenge for you. Take what you've learned and put it into action.

- Start by setting a savings goal. Maybe you want to save money for a new toy or a special trip.

- Create a budget to help you reach that goal.

- Talk to your family about what you've learned. Share your goals and ask for their advice.

- And don't forget to be generous. Find a way to help someone else, whether it's by donating to a charity or volunteering your time.

From my heart to yours, I want you to know that this journey has been as exciting for me as I hope it was for you. Having shared these lessons with many children and students, I've seen firsthand how important it is to start learning about money early. And now, you have the chance to start saving early and help secure your financial future.

Remember, you have the power to make smart choices. You can earn, save, spend, and give wisely. These skills will help you not just now but for the rest of your life. You're already on the path to being a money master. Keep learning, keep saving, and keep helping others. Your future is bright, and I'm so proud of you for taking these steps.

So go out there and make your money work for you. Whether you're saving for a new bike, planning a fun family trip, or just making sure you're not tricked by scammers, you've got this. And always remember, the best part of having money is not just what you can buy but how it can help you and others live better lives!

Thank you for joining me on this journey. Keep dreaming big, keep working hard, and, most importantly, keep being kind and generous. The world needs more smart, savvy, and kind-hearted kids like you.

Happy saving, and good luck!

With love and best wishes,

Catherine Louis

Chapter 11

Keeping the Game Alive

Congratulations! You now have the tools you need to start earning, saving, and spending wisely. But the journey doesn't stop here.

Now, it's your turn to pass on what you've learned.

By leaving your honest opinion of this book on Amazon, you can help other kids just like you find the same money skills and confidence you've gained. Think of it as sharing a secret treasure map that leads to financial success!

Your review will:

- Guide other kids toward helpful tips on saving and spending.

- Show families where to find fun, easy-to-understand money advice.

- Inspire future entrepreneurs to start their journeys.

Thank you for helping keep the *Money Skills for Young Minds* mission alive. When we share what we know, we all grow smarter together.

Please scan this code to leave a review-

- Your support means the world. Thank you for being part of this adventure!

With gratitude, *Catherine Louis*

Other books by Catherine Louis that you may be interested in:

Self-Love for Teen Girls: An Empowering Guide to Release and Sustain Your Confidence, Resilience, and Emotional Well-Being Without the Overwhelm

https://www.amazon.com/Self-Love-Teen-Girls-Empowering-Confidence/dp/B0CY8T1R1C/-18

Powerful Skills for Teens and Young Adults: Easily Master Time Management, Communication, and Financial Literacy. Develop Goals and Relationships So You Thrive Plus More

https://www.amazon.com/Powerful-Skills-Teens-Young-Adults/dp/B0DDJJRQFD